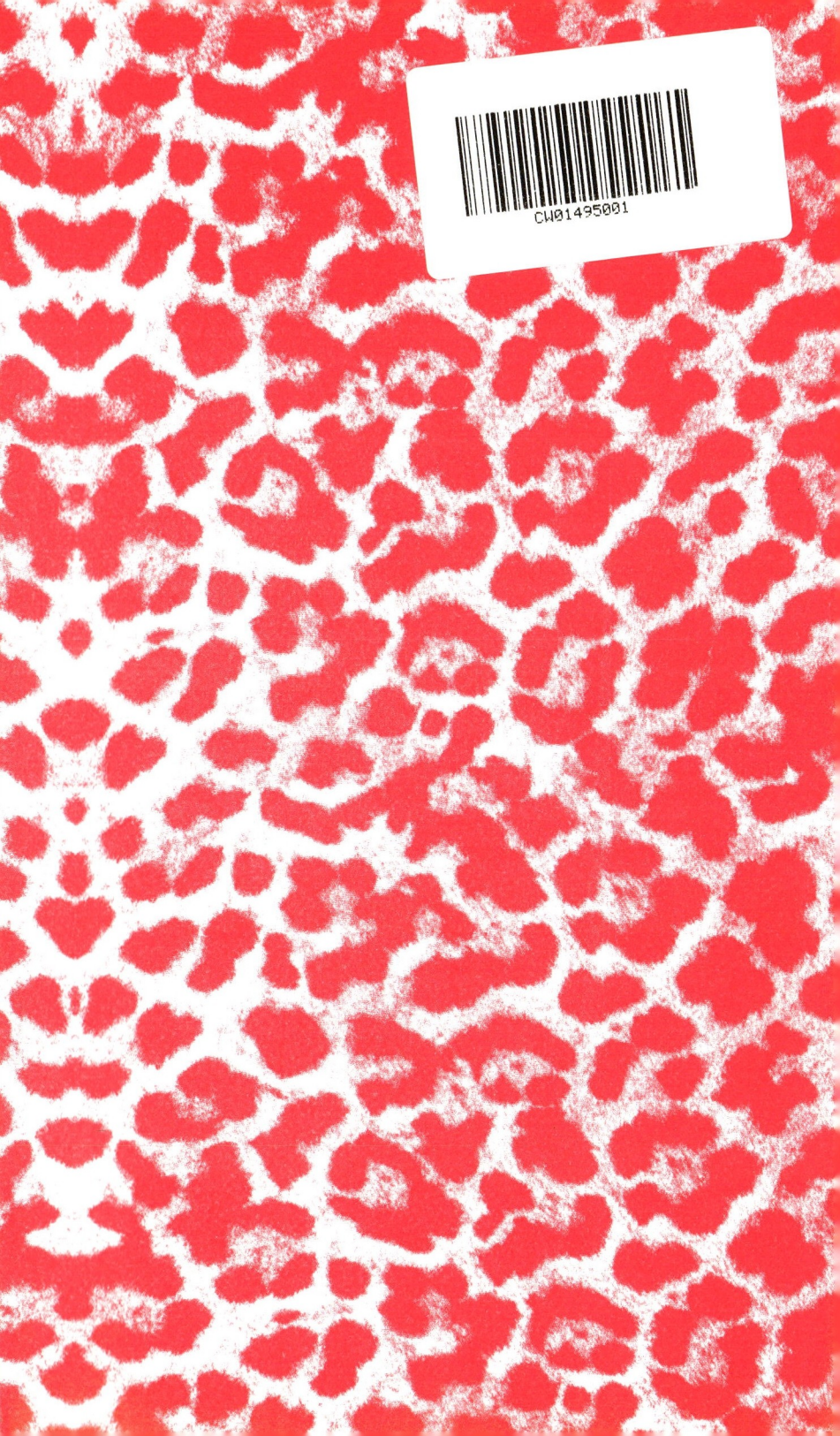

BAD TASTE

BAD TASTE

Or the Politics of Ugliness

NATHALIE OLAH

dialogue
books

DIALOGUE BOOKS

First published in Great Britain in 2023 by Dialogue Books

10 9 8 7 6 5 4 3 2

A CIP catalogue record for this book
is available from the British Library.

Hardback ISBN 978-0-3497-0226-1
Trade paperback ISBN 978-0-3497-0225-4

Typeset in Berling by M Rules
Printed and bound in Great Britain by
Clays Ltd, Elcograf S.p.A

Papers used by Dialogue Books are from well-managed forests
and other responsible sources.

Dialogue Books
Carmelite House
50 Victoria Embankment
London EC4Y 0DZ

Dialogue Books, part of Little Brown, Book Group Limited,
an Hachette UK company

www.dialoguebooks.co.uk

For Brian Smith

Contents

Chapter One

Tastemakers

> Consider the exact sense in which a work of art is said to be 'in good or bad taste'. It does not mean that it is true or false; that it is beautiful or ugly; but that it does or does not comply either with the laws of choice which are enforced by certain modes of life, or the habits of mind produced by a particular sort of education.
>
> JOHN RUSKIN, *Modern Painters*, volume III (1888)

> To me, bad taste is what entertainment is all about. If someone vomits watching one of my films, it's like getting a standing ovation.
>
> JOHN WATERS, *Shock Value* (1981)

Two Johns, as unalike as any two people could be, yet preoccupied by the same subject: *taste*, or what governs our likes and dislikes. Ruskin, the nineteenth-century polymath and critic, and Waters, the *énfant terrible* of late-twentieth-century film-making, responsible for such classics as *Pink Flamingos* (1972), *Hairspray* (1988), and *Cry-Baby* (1990), might not belong to the same wheelhouse or even the same universe. Where Waters did much to free the pubic hair in sex scenes in which it abounds, Ruskin purportedly demurred from its presence on his wife's body, leading to the annulment of their marriage (in what might be the most widely told, and widely discredited, urban legend in all of art history). Between these two quotations, however, exists a neat summary of how my own attitudes towards matters of taste have evolved over time. What once inspired resistance and disdain in me, per Waters, still does, only now it is joined by an element of curiosity for the social forces that are driving that disdain, per Ruskin. The weight of conforming to ideas of good taste, which I always sought to overcome by presenting as scruffy or abject, has finally evolved into a matter of inquiry.

This first started to happen through my loose involvement in various political causes. Travelling outside of London, where I live, and observing the interactions between people who stood to gain far more from understanding each other than not, but who were nevertheless divided along superficial lines strangely predicated on what the other was wearing, how they styled their hair, or how they had chosen to design their homes, I decided a book on this subject was needed. Time and time again, expectations about the wealth, lifestyles and political allegiances of the other were being proven wrong, as unlikely conversations were being struck up between people who were forced to admit the failure of their judgements. Stereotypes of a small-minded, petit bourgeois existence that had been the subject of countless internet memes – Fiat 500 cars and *Live, Laugh, Love* wall hangings – were no more a guarantee of someone's conservative values, it turns out, than pink hair, septum piercings and a push-bike were an indication of the opposite. The culture wars that had been confected by certain political leaders, and amplified by the media, had created a climate in which all of us had been reduced to our appearances, and in a way that was impeding our ability to discern the truth.

Many of my peers have turned away from this subject, and for good reason: no one wants to be accused of dwelling on the trivialities that undermine our politics. But to ignore what I witnessed on doorsteps and in community halls, is to ignore certain conditions that allowed for these culture wars to be mounted in the first place. Through reading Ruskin and others, I came to understand how ideas of taste might be connected to wealth and power, forming one of the more emotional, and socially ostracising, dimensions of the class system in which we live.

I have found that this kind of statement is, however, sometimes misinterpreted, and used to falsely justify the vilification of artists and intellectuals. To make a slight alter-ation on Ruskin's statement, in a contemporary context at least, I believe 'education' and 'modes of life' produce slightly different outcomes, and want to state from the beginning the difference between taste and expertise. Disciplines are not elitist for the fact that they require learning: it is not true to say that art or literature, or any other discipline for that matter, is exclusionary because an understanding of it requires time and effort (although it is fair to say that spare time and effort are often only readily available to the wealthy, but more on that later). Such a belief – that specialist subjects represent a kind of tyranny – leads to the assumption made by egotistical celebrities, for example, that they can simply turn their hand to art (apparently asking themselves, *How difficult can it be?* Well, quite, it would seem, if you have ever gazed upon a painting by any number of actors and former musicians who have tried to sell us their paintings). It also leads to the demand for work by people like Damien Hirst, who has embraced a mass-produced, art-as-commerce model, similar in ethos (though crucially lacking the same ingenuity with respect to social commentary), to the work of the pop artists half a century earlier; or those algorithm-generated Bored Ape NFTs that the rich were parading around with dumb pride about a year ago.

What is elitist, exclusionary and a legitimate cause of grievance, in my opinion, is the weaponisation of second-hand knowledge by people, consumers to be more precise, who are not experts on a given subject, but derive a sense of superiority from having learned a set of rules with which to simulate knowledge. It is the reduction of learning to aesthetic codes. Or to put it more bluntly, it is 'good taste' masquerading as culture.

These rules, codes, or however else we might want to describe the good taste dictates that so many people live by, and which I have used to subtitle each chapter of this book, are usually connected to matters of lifestyle and consumerism, and constitute *the done thing*, without anyone needing to understand or explain exactly why. And while this bigotry might seem innocent on the face of it, with no real consequences for anyone involved, part of writing this book is to highlight how ideas of taste might in fact contain, and also protect and normalise, a great number of stubborn and harmful prejudices.

When I discuss this fixation with matters of taste, I am referring to the tendency distilled by magazines such as *How to Spend It*, published weekly by the *Financial Times* and whose name so perfectly encapsulates the blind march of late capitalism, and the need to earn more and more for reasons that often elude the participant, as to appear almost beautiful to me, even poetic. Wild and empty and hollow as it might be, nailing the art of consumerism seems to be the thing that drives millions of people to push harder, to strive more and to see their fellow men, and fellow workers, as points of competition and one-upmanship, rather than the friends and allies that they ought to be – and by reverse, to denigrate and ridicule others. The insecurity and shame born of that dynamic is one that is ripe for exploitation by those who thrive on division, allowing them to mount campaigns that can feel reassuringly loud, rambunctious and incendiary.

I am guilty as anyone of soothing myself with assurances about my own superior aesthetic judgement, but have also felt at times victimised by that same tendency. It is for this reason that throughout this book I will draw on a combination of experience and research. Because tens, if not hundreds, of moments flood the memory when I begin to think of the many ways in which I first rebelled against, and then reluctantly conformed to, ideas of good taste in order to survive. Not being born into wealth, I understood early on that my security depended on being able to emulate the social mores and preferences of those in power: school teachers, university admissions staff, job recruiters, bank managers and letting agents. But to describe any one of these encounters in much detail would be dull, and almost too obvious. What is more interesting to me are the ways in which matters of taste shaped even my earliest memories, and how fundamental to my worldview they must have always been.

The sanctuary of trash

The story begins, then, in the video store of Rubery High Street in South Birmingham, near to my grandmother's house where I spent much of my childhood. The video store is one of those redundant entities that has a way of emphasising the passage of time. Life today might not look that different to how it did thirty years ago, at least in Britain, but the video store is one of the few exceptions, and really carries the quaint parochialism of a bygone age. Younger readers might pity those of us born before 2000, who had to physically browse the aisles, select a case, have the store attendant scurry off into their little storage room to fill the case with its corresponding cassette, and then had to post that same cassette through a little hatch in the store's front door a few days later. Nothing could have seemed more intoxicating to my seven-year-old self, however, standing among the towering shelves of that particular video store and its portal to a Hollywood dreamscape of orange skies and neon aphorisms. The store was small, always very dark, and staffed by teenagers who seemed impossibly worldly to me, one of whom, a friend of my aunt's, was saving her earnings to become a flight attendant and a permanent fixture of those orange skies.

At that time a cardboard cut-out of Pamela Anderson had

appeared in front of the main counter as part of a campaign to promote the action film *Barb Wire* (1996). A poster was hung next to it carrying the film's slogan – 'Don't Call Me Babe!' – in large, black, sans-serif type set against a white background. In both, Anderson wore a skin-tight satin and PVC bodysuit and stiletto heels, breasts nuzzled together like the two bread rolls that I carried in a plastic bag from the bakery a few doors down, as she raised her arms to wield a 357 Desert Eagle. I was trailing my mom as she said her hellos to the staff, who were some of her friends, when my eyes rested on this image that caught my attention in ways that few things have ever since. When asked what I wanted to rent, I said, '*That.*' And while there was something libidinal at play, while I was certainly attracted to the beautiful woman with bitchy over-drawn lip liner and a big explosion of blonde hair, it was also the severity of the image, the polarities of yellow hair dye and black lycra, the cutesy, baby-doll face rendered severe thanks to the needle-point eyebrows, lavish winged eyeshadow and frosted lip gloss, that got me. It was an image that resisted any kind of softness, which has its virtues, of course, but being raised as a girl in a world that I had already understood demanded a gentleness and a prettiness of me – whose entire schooling, even at the tender age of seven and at the inner-city state school I attended, was more invested in helping me to iron out the 'coarser' parts of my nature than imparting knowledge of any kind – this image represented a kind of freedom. As did the evident discomfort it inspired in almost everyone who stepped inside, forming a sort of void at the heart of the video store that people learned to step aside and avert their eyes from.

For me, this encounter recalls the story told by Dolly

Parton, in which she describes her first encounter with the style that would eventually become her signature. Speaking to CBS News in 2006, Parton explained: 'There was this woman that was very much a loose woman. I didn't know what that meant, and I just told her how beautiful she was, 'cause she had this beautiful yellow hair. She left a big impression on me, and I would talk about how beautiful she was and different ones would say, "Oh, she's just trash." And I thought, "That's what I want to be when I grow up. I'm gonna be trash!"'[1] For the people made to feel like trash already by a system of inequality, or widespread discrimination in the form of misogyny, racism and homophobia, reclaiming trashiness as an identity can be powerful. I realise now that all of my early friendships were defined by this, as I sought out people who felt themselves to be excluded from a system of quiet social dominance and power centred within the white, middle-class tradition, and who found comfort instead in being able to find alternative modes of expression that might offend it. I believe this was only propelled by the very particular climate in which we were living, and a moment in history that placed so much stock on professional appearances and respectability.

Dr Frasier Winslow Crane, MD, PhD, APA

One show, *Frasier*, went further than most to mock this tendency and was popular among parents of the time in which I was growing up. A spin-off of the earlier sitcom *Cheers!*, created by David Angell, Peter Casey and David Lee and starring comedian Kelsey Grammer, who played the show's titular character Frasier Crane – a somewhat celebrated, somewhat wealthy psychiatrist and radio host living in Seattle – it is a show whose entire comic premise hinges on the question of good taste: the joke being that both Frasier and his younger brother Niles, also a psychiatrist – two highly qualified and expensively educated men responsible for the wellbeing of other people – remain incapable of reconciling their bourgeois anxieties with the no-nonsense conditions of an upbringing at the hands of Martin, their father and the show's primary agitator, who is forced to live with Frasier after an accident compromises his mobility.

Martin, or Marty as he is often referred to throughout the show, is a retired blue-collar cop who favours objects and activities that provide comfort and light relief. His sons, who owe much of their sensibility to their deceased mother Hester, who was also a psychiatrist, favour objects and activities that provide edification and sublime reverie: opera, fine wines, the works of Dostoyevsky, the 'Goldberg Variations', Eames chairs and other notable objects of mid-century design, fine art, women with bobs, cheeses and place settings. The show does not suggest that there is anything wrong with these items or activities in and of themselves, but simply mocks the status anxiety that attends them. Marty, by contrast, is characterised by a relaxed love of his lint-speckled recliner chair, plaid shirts, steak-house visits, canned beer and his dog, Eddie, a Jack Russell terrier played by a celebrated dog actor named Moose. This was an apt choice of breed it turns out, given the show's themes, as the Jack Russell terrier had been subject to its own version of a class struggle in the 1990s, with a fierce debate raging in the American Kennel Club at the time as to the dog's status and function: traditionalists arguing for the Jack Russell to remain a working dog and bred accordingly, while a growing (and ultimately victorious) contingent fought hard for it to be further domesticated and made more amenable to the home.

Eddie's face-offs with Frasier are a tacit communication of the struggle for Martin's affections, as Frasier's snobbish rebellions reveal themselves to be a rebuttal of that first and far more profound rejection, in not being 'man' enough to fulfil the expectations of a father who had worked in the police force. But these two breeds – the university-educated professional upstart and the Jack Russell terrier – shared many similarities at the end of the last century, with both being forced to navigate a brave new world of greater comfort on the one hand, but also a new set of expectations in how they must behave on the other.

Frasier first aired in September 1993 and at a time of hope for great swathes of America. Bill Clinton assumed the presidency in January that year, and his programme of Third Way liberal economic reforms would alleviate some of the inequality imposed by his predecessor, the Republican George Bush Sr. If George Bush Sr had exemplified the acumen and steely void of personality marked by his previous profession as a businessman – and if *his* predecessor, Ronald Reagan, had embodied the even more bland and hollow spectacle of the light entertainer and showman – then Clinton had the relaxed, jocular air and self-effacing quality of the supremely well-educated. A Rhodes scholar and qualified lawyer with certificates from Georgetown, Oxford and Yale, Clinton's approach seemed to be rooted in a sober-minded pragmatism backed up by the books, a man motivated by gentle reforms towards inclusive social values, greater equality and an enlarged middle class. It was an agenda that, on appearances at least, served as an antidote to the more mercenary, money-making tendencies that had defined the atmosphere of public life throughout the 1980s.

On the campaign trail in 1992 – an event I do not remember, but one that would set the tone for the Clinton presidency, which I definitely do, being as it was completely inescapable throughout the 1990s – both Bill and Hillary are captured in various looks distinct in their slouchiness from the rather more formal attire of their predecessors. Bill wears patterned ties and loose-fitting, single-breasted suits, often undoing the buttons or removing the jacket altogether while Hillary wears a variety of brightly coloured, monochromatic outfits and velvet hairbands, beneath which her hair enjoys a hitherto unknown level of abandon for a would-be First Lady, without any apparent help from mousse, hair gel or spray. On a couple of occasions Hillary also wears an over-sized leather bomber jacket, while on the night of Clinton's win, daughter Chelsea wears a polka-dot sailor-style dress of a type that might be encountered on a Varsity trip to France. It is a theme that would run throughout the Clinton presidency, of Chelsea wearing long, oversized floral dresses befitting a homestead in Western Europe, before graduating onto the rather more formal skirt suit, and echoing her parents whose entire ethos was about blurring the line between stiff formality and *everyday life*. It was important that the family oozed a sense of relaxed ease, and an almost pastoral vision of modern America, where education reforms would ensure that good sense prevailed. The two students who had supposedly met on a picket line in 1971 were still detectable in the softer, more tactile outline of Bill and Hillary's clothing, which came to define many fashions of the time.

Of all the characters included in the cast of *Cheers!* none was more suited to carrying a spin-off show in the early 1990s than Frasier Crane, who in spite of the leading actor's own personal inclinations towards Republicanism, perfectly encapsulated the very specific strain of status anxiety that the Democratic Party presided over and which gripped the nation; one that was concerned as much with erudition, as with wealth. Coincidentally, Frasier's aptly named wife Lilith Sternin bore a resemblance to one of America's best-known female intellectuals of the time, Donna Tartt, whose hit novel *The Secret History* was published in the year prior to *Frasier* being aired. Frasier epitomised the new, slightly fusty economic group whose creation defined the era, in his uniform of itchy-looking woollen suits, occasional waistcoats and, during the *Cheers!* years at least, experimentations in facial hair that the commercial lawyer or trader of the 1980s could only have dreamed of. As with Clinton, Frasier was averse to all forms of product to tame the head hair, which in both men's cases enjoyed a certain fluffiness of texture.

This was the fashionable ambience of the world I grew up in, which my parents and their friends sought to emulate in whatever charity shop or hand-me-down approximations they could get their hands on. We were living in an era of oversized cardigans and corduroy trousers, waistcoats and no-nonsense, straight-cut jeans, men with small hoop earrings and women with chestnut-coloured hair. If Tartt's novel sky-rocketed the campus format, then around it came a slew of enormously popular films where the campus, formal education or the idea of 'genius' was central, among them *Peter's Friends* (1992), *Circle of Friends* (1995), and *Good Will Hunting* (1997). Friends – in the general sense, but also in the popular TV show of the same name, of course – were inescapable. Had the notion even formally existed before the cultural output of the 1990s, or much like the teenager of the 1950s, do we owe our contemporary understanding of this word to an era in which every story seemed to centre on lifelong, platonic affinities forged in the university common room, or shortly thereafter?

Regardless, it was always autumn, or fall, in the 1990s, and the boulevards of our imagination were lined with maple trees, as everyone, on some level, attended Harvard. If Chelsea wore a sailor dress to Clinton's inauguration, then the wedding of my mother and father – an event of similar magnitude, at least to those of us who knew them – would require me to wear the same. Where Chelsea's was blue, mine would be yellow, or 'lemon' as I apparently stipulated to the shop assistant in Laura Ashley. At Christmas time we would take the money my mother had saved and spend it on velvet coats bought from the department store in town, while in the hairdresser's that played Bobby Brown's 'Two Can Play That Game' at full volume, my mum cut her hair into a neat crop that said *studious, but sexy*.

And things didn't end at personal style. Of course, one of the main adjustments in the evolution from *Cheers!* to *Frasier* was shifting the focal point from the bar, presided over by Ted Danson's character Sam in *Cheers!*, to Frasier's home, where the set would serve to illuminate many of the show's central themes. Arguably its fourth most significant character, whose symbolism spoke to us with a biting humour, the show's post-modern set design, famously incorporating vast, panoramic windows with views over the city of Seattle, a semi-circular hearth, various mid-century-design items – including an Eames lounger, but also various objects of importance from sub-Saharan Africa in the totemic and problematic way of Freud, a grand piano and smooth glass tabletops – is as perfect a distillation as any created for the screen, of an aspirational, 1990s eclecticism: the *what, this old thing?* bearer of luxury that indicated an extensive knowledge of art and culture, and an even more extensive stock of air miles. Almost a century earlier, economist Thorstein Veblen had posited his theory of 'the leisure class', 'conspicuous consumption' and 'conspicuous leisure' in which he observed a tendency among the wealthy capitalists created by nineteenth-century industrialism to demonstrate their social standing through items that provided evidence of a life that was rich in experience. Where the aristocrat had proudly displayed his golden candelabras and oil paintings, the new wealth created by the opportunities of free-market capitalism often tended to be displayed more in the demonstration of proficiencies and travel, through sporting trophies or souvenirs, for example. The *Frasier* set, then, was also an expression of far-reaching adventures, be those literary or actual: the home of someone who enjoyed mini-breaks, gallery visits, magazine subscriptions and recipe cards, and would be adept at navigating the sorts of conversations one could expect to encounter at dinner parties among equally affluent friends.

The genius of *Frasier* was in identifying a phenomenon

taking place across America – of certain demographics being freed from traditional class hierarchies, not so much through business and commerce, but through education, and families whose previous generations had been consigned at birth to a certain level of income and prosperity finding hope – but also tension – in the resulting opportunities. Perhaps the excitement of the era was nowhere more evident than in the extreme flights of fancy permitted by domestic dramas and comedies of the time – more bizarre and otherworldly than any science fiction in their assertion that even under this new set of circumstances, aspiring authors and paralegals might afford to rent spacious real estate in the centre of major US cities. Yet *Frasier* got around this problem by dealing with characters who had already made it, and gave the impression, one vindicated through time, of being far more knowing about the seismic shifts taking place around it than contemporaries *Friends*, *Ally McBeal*, *Sex and the City* or *Seinfeld*.

If I had first seen my parents watching *Frasier* in the 1990s, chuckling to themselves over jokes I did not understand, then by the time I returned to it, on the laptop that was propped up on my single bed in the tiny room that I rented in a flat that I shared with my two friends Lydia and Nicole in East London in the early 2010s, then I was forming my own, somewhat jaded opinions about the professional world. At twenty-one I had a degree to my name and several years' work experience, yet found myself much less employable than I had imagined. Few experiences can be so conducive to converting people to the cause of left-wing politics than allowing them to spend three years among 'peers', who on re-entering normal life reveal themselves to be anything but; the academic qualifications attained paling in comparison to family connections and independent wealth. Ironically for someone who had just spent three years studying English novels, I found myself in a position similar to that of a nineteenth-century governess, and only then came to understand why this figure had been so useful to its authors, creating as it did endless narrative possibilities. For three years I worked as its nearest modern-day equivalent, the tutor and nanny, travelling around London and beyond, traipsing through the homes of affluent families and enjoying a freedom of movement that would have otherwise been impossible. During the hundreds of visits made to these homes, and much like the characters of the Oscar-winning film *Parasite* (2019), I would sometimes find myself unattended in vast mansions, spying sad, despondent mums, drunk dads, and – on a couple of occasions – caught children taking large quantities of mephedrone in the privacy of their bedrooms.

As such, I also started to identify (as much as anyone can identify with what I believe to be the most thinly drawn and stereotypical of all the show's characters) with Daphne Moon, Martin's carer, Frasier's housekeeper, and fittingly, the show's Mancunian voice of reason. As a domestic labourer, Daphne shares many of the older Crane's beliefs and attitudes, as well as a healthy degree of cynicism towards the vanity of the two Crane brothers. If *Frasier* is the promise that was sold to aspiring university graduates of the 1990s and 2000s, then for many of us in the wake of the 2008 financial crisis, Daphne was the reality. Though unlike her, whose relentless optimism in the face of low pay and the three men's unreasonable demands might be added to the list of unrealistic details in

US sitcoms of the time, my own attitude was one of comparative cynicism. Among the frequent humiliation and minimal remuneration, the many Frasierisms I encountered daily were the one source of entertainment to be found in these jobs, and without my knowing it at the time, they had inducted me into a literary tradition that included the Brontës and Lucia Berlin.

By observing these affluent people in their homes, I was able to gain some understanding of the connection drawn between taste and prosperity in the minds of the wealthy. Among the absurdities I encountered, none remain so vivid to me as a house transformed by its owner into a sort of art gallery, whose walls were completely devoid of colour and whose only apparent concession to the children who lived there was in the shape of four large bowls containing exclusively white jelly sweets. To me, the children were impossible to discipline and seemed preoccupied with chaos. It was here that I encountered a life-size, figurative sculpture by a notable British artist, that appeared like an intruder every time you entered the room, and which only exacerbated what I perceived to be the neuroses of a family that had consigned itself to a glass house containing several million pounds worth of art.

Until that point in my life, however, no place could have seemed more luxurious or aspirational, and the idea of having famous artworks on display seemed to be the absolute pinnacle of prosperity. But after being invited to teach in the home of an old American dynastic family, whose house in a smart area of London was set among far fewer modernist buildings (which the owners unsurprisingly loathed), I learned that older wealth was displayed through possessions of an inherited variety, as I sat uncomfortably eating pancakes supplied by a maid, among endless silverware and Ming dynasty objects. Then further on, in the home of an aristocrat and lawyer, I learned that any concern for taste was vulgar and one should be free to 'slum it', while being given cracked branded mugs of tea in the garden room of a sixteenth-century villa. A similar tendency was on display in a photograph shared by the Royal Family's social media account in 2021 of the interior at Gatcombe Park in Gloucestershire, the residence of Princess Anne, Queen Elizabeth II's daughter. The photograph showed the princess and her husband Sir Timothy Laurence enjoying a game of rugby via their TV set, surrounded by a variety of mis-matched furniture, much of it cluttered with various ornaments and framed photographs, artworks of various kinds and in various styles of frame, armchairs and sofas bearing a complex floral print, and a dog bed. The scene is typical of any upper-middle-class household in Britain, and yet countless op-eds seemed to drum up incredulity, failing to make the point as always, that power and respectability often enjoy an inverse relationship, and that conformity to ideas of tastefulness is often a requirement handed down to the lower classes as a necessity for entry to the halls of financial security, while the wealthy are free to live like pigs.[2]

On reflection, and in my opinion at least, I did visit one house where the owners had put their money to good use, design-wise. This was the home of a wealthy businessman originally from India whose entire aesthetic sensibility had evolved outside of the world of the white British middle class – a mansion again in West London – that contained a continuous mural covering its four vast floors. From one room to the next there ran an elaborate scene in saccharine pastel colours, of pergolas, trailing creepers, winding streams and roaming fauna.

My own domestic setting was also replete with roaming fauna at that time. Mice would appear on our pillows at night and run along the poorly fitted skirting board, and only after a year did I discover the resident python my housemate had been keeping in her room, after a chance encounter in the hallway. Social media was relatively new. Magazines were popping up every few months with distinctive new styles that would garner a few thousand 'followers', most of whom lived in a one-mile radius of our flat. People were starting to 'post' about their lives online, sharing glimpses from parties, travels and the books that they were reading. 'Curated' as a verb started to acquire a broader spectrum of meaning beyond the work carried out by an art gallery professional, as we were all being called upon to curate our lives via the Internet.

Online validation would emerge as a possible curative for the real-world misery felt by the jobless and the skint, who would accrue small collections of earthenware pots, linocut prints of morbid faces, chrysanthemums, paperweights and pens, all of which were photographed and shared. It was hardly the spoils of the Frasier Crane residence, but during the 'Great Recession', we constructed our little shrines to respectability in the corners of the single bedrooms rented in shared houses, posting them online for the likes that had replaced the other, real-world forms of interaction and validation that existed before.

Rise of the tastemakers

These online profiles formed part of an emerging economy of images whose nuclei would be found a few miles left of the financial centres governing the flow of global capital – in the places where advertisers, marketeers and influencers were congregating under the pretence of creativity. Tastefulness, as an idea and as a lifestyle, had become the stock-in-trade of a new type of business that was harnessing the proliferation in visual media. At the same time, an emphasis on the personal and the cultural, as it pertained to image, was being validated in the halls of professional attainment and financial security. During this time, I applied for countless positions at IT firms, political organisations, NGOs and magazines – anything to get me out of the nannying – most of which, at some point in the recruitment process, required some public declaration of a self that had shown itself to be aware of the cultural sensibilities and preferences of those in charge, be it through blogging or the creation of a professional online profile.

Rather than lacking the right qualifications, or being unable to fulfil the practical duties of a role, on more than one occasion I was also rejected on the grounds of being a poor 'cultural fit'; a strange term, probably being used euphemistically, of course, but whose legitimacy nevertheless seemed to indicate that the former pretence of an unbiased and pragmatic professional sphere – but also the pretence of a work/life distinction – had been eroded. Culture, which had always been conceived of as a personal matter divorced from someone's work, had somehow found its way into the world of employment criteria. On the one hand, recruiters were under more pressure than ever to avoid explicit forms of discrimination, with job forms that contained drop-down menus that insisted on asking for details as to one's race, gender, sexual preference or religious beliefs. But elsewhere and in formats that were much less traceable, but much more intimidating – in interviews that were being held more frequently over coffee, or even drinks, and with people being subject to lengthy processes, sometimes being grilled by panels of people for the allocation of a minimum-wage job – a stronger emphasis than ever before was being placed on *who we were* and *how we spent our free time*. As Ashley Mears has pointed out, increasingly companies are seeking employees who embody the right 'look'[4], where the right look encompasses everything from physical appearance (which Mears refers to specifically here), to style of dress, conversational manner, and the places one might be seen in the hours after clocking off. Elsewhere, and in another case of work cannibalising our personal lives and requiring the demonstration of good taste, the rise of gig economy work necessitated that service providers such as Uber drivers and TaskRabbit handymen create profiles with a picture, and in the case of some other services, even a short bio, while customers were free to rank them according to a set of undefined criteria. This meant that style of dress, personal smell, preferred topic of conversation and choice of music could be the difference between a five- or one-star rating, and by extension, the difference between securing further work or not. In any customer-facing job, questions of taste dictate employability, and this I would venture has only become more pronounced in an age where feedback is registered online instantly and to such devastating effect.

In 1977, Pierre Bourdieu and Jean-Claude Passeron coined the term 'cultural capital' to refer to the cultural knowledge and social assets that endear people to those in power. This included education and manner of speech, but also style of dress, aesthetic preference and lifestyle. Aspects of cultural capital might be bestowed at birth, or acquired in the course of a person's life. However, that process of acquisition, which can be long, painful and alienating, is often also determined by the person's proximity (socially, ideologically and also geographically) to the dominant culture, putting immigrants, and people of an opposing faith, ethnicity or style of education at a disadvantage. This is all without even mentioning the cultural erasure that takes place as a result.

Bourdieu and Passeron's theory showed how a labour system that reduces people to their commodity value makes an economic attribute of certain tendencies and preferences. *Frasier* parodied this, not by mocking education or so-called high culture for their own sake, but their transformation into a economic asset that a person might trade. What seemed apparent to me, however, is that the situation had evolved, and that the anxieties related to cultural capital that *Frasier* dealt in in the 1990s were also becoming increasingly systematised and coded into a person's identity, or at least that of their online avatar, on account of developments in work and technology.

It is important to acknowledge as well, that in addition to the snobbish traits of the main character and his brother, *Frasier* also considered the ways in which formerly niche disciplines were being popularised through new forms of media. This was not incidental to the matter of cultural capital, but arguably central to it. Broadcasting had transformed countless specialist disciplines into forms of light entertainment, and their practitioners into celebrities and performers. In Frasier's transformation from a psychotherapist into a psychotherapist-cum-radio-host, the show detailed a wider trend for radio and TV programming that sought to resolve matters of personal suffering and interpersonal conflict publicly, most harmfully perhaps in the form of the *Jerry Springer* and *Ricki Lake* shows, or *The Jeremy Kyle Show* in the UK. But there was a tendency to make an entertaining spectacle of almost any profession, with the emergence of so many TV and radio doctors, astronomers, historians, lawyers and judges, but also chefs, interior designers and artists. Frasier frequently grappled with the anxiety of maintaining a certain image, but also the problem of discrediting his profession by reducing it to a consumable soundbite. As a sort of proto-podcaster, he exemplified a set of anxieties that would only become more widespread with the proliferation in new media channels, the advent of social media, and the ability of almost anyone to become a self-styled expert and semi-public figure. The Clinton years would seem to spell a time of great respect for education, academia and expertise, but the greater remuneration for these disciplines was on the condition that they also be made more commercially viable and subsumed into the market economy: academics, doctors and other such experts, being transformed into businessmen and performers. Subjects for which even a basic level of comprehension required years of study were being presented to the public in a way that suggested they might be 'got' by consuming a short radio or TV segment, thereby promoting the false idea that *looking* and *hearing* are equivalent to *understanding*.

We were being coaxed into a state of accepting everything at the face value of the screen (or the speaker), and at the same time faced with the fact of having to optimise ourselves for these channels in order to succeed. By the time we had reached the early 2010s, the tendency had reached a cacophony. In 2010, the CEO of Google Eric Schmidt admitted that we create as much information in two days now 'as we did from the dawn of man through 2003'.[5] Loath as I am to quote any executive of Google, this admission goes some way to confirming that our lives are now peculiarly saturated with images, soundbites and data. It has almost become too plain a fact to state – almost a cliché – that those of us in possession of a smartphone, laptop or tablet, but also those living in a town or city where advertising space is inescapable, are being supplied more visual information daily than we could ever process properly. This might be via photographs, videos or the formats that exist somewhere in between – GIFs, reels, montages – posted in the billions every single day. In such a climate, the will and capacity to discern truth from appearances will be eroded. We are being led into a situation where impressions reign supreme.

This is really the fulfilment of what the French philosopher and artist Guy Debord termed *The Society of the Spectacle*, and particularly the idea that in the age of the spectacle, the 'social relation between people ... is mediated by images.'[6] The observations made by Debord, and other twentieth-century writers of a similar tradition – among them Jacques Derrida, Susan Sontag and Stuart Hall – have only become more relevant with time, and in many ways our reality is one that they all, variously, predicted: where presentation is not only important to the outcome of a person's life, but in many ways, paramount. Perhaps it was easier for them, living in the dawn of so much visual technology, to observe its transformative effects, than it is for those of us today, living in a world created by it.

A note on phrasing

Each of these writers was careful about their wording, and in that same vein I am required to just make one final note on the language that I will use throughout this book. *Class* by the Marxist definition refers to our relationship to capital – those who own the land, the buildings, the machinery and the equipment required to produce goods (what is referred to as *the means of production*), constitute the capitalist and ruling class. The people dependent on them for wage labour constitute the workers. Capitalists take profit from the wealth that is created by workers. This definition, however, ran into some difficulty with the creation of new types of work in the twentieth century, including those based in services and which engage digital technology, in which it became harder to ascertain what we were producing, how we were creating wealth and who was in possession of the often-intangible resources on which it all depended. Today there is an ongoing debate as to whether the middle or capitalist class is defined as those able to save, who own property or who make at least part of their income passively, through the renting out of property, or through the ownership of shares, for example. It is not that the class system ceased to exist, but that our definitions needed to be modernised. Nevertheless, right-wing politicians have seized on this confusion to argue that we now live in a fair society with no class differences, thereby disguising the stubborn inequalities of wealth which have nevertheless persisted. Their big lie was that we now lived in a *meritocracy* – that is, a society that operates by fairness and rewards people according to their efforts – and that a person's earnings were tied to their virtues and their character.

In this new world, 'class' became a word that was maligned and corrupted. A term that had once described the conditions imposed by a system of capital, was increasingly used to denote a facet of personality. The earliest instances of 'class' being used synonymously with 'refinement' might have derived from the shortening of something being 'first rate' or indeed 'first class', rather than having any socioeconomic basis. But over time this converged with the other definition of blue- and white-collar workers, or the rich and poor. Thanks to American TV shows, 'class' became something a person either had or didn't have. As a broad term it could be applied to many situations, with the 'classy' often being those who demonstrated poise and an unwillingness to engage in petty arguments, but also those who demonstrated elegance with respect to their appearances and homes. In that case, those who had *class* were more often than not also people who were already doing well, and their prosperity was understood to be a reward for that virtue. If a person wasn't doing well, it was because they *lacked* this virtue, the virtue of *class*, and their impoverishment was judged to be the external manifestation of a rotten character, too chaotic and disordered to warrant reward in the theatre of hand-outs.

The word *taste* underwent a similar evolution. A term of no implied value became shorthand for 'good taste', and again, one either possessed taste, or didn't. It was not a case of this being my taste and that being yours, but a hierarchy whose ascent could only be achieved by hanging around the right people, reading the right magazines and exposing oneself to the right strains of culture. By this definition, 'taste' came to refer to a person's ability to successfully emulate the aesthetic codes of those in power. Taste and class converged. To have taste, was to have class, was to have understood the social codes enforced by the protectors of money and opportunity. While to lack taste, was to lack class, was to serve as grounds for social derision and economic exclusion. The adjustment in meaning was slight but profound, from the stratification of society due to the extraction of wealth by a powerful few, to a personal quality and aspect of character whose absence is the result of some personal and moral failing. Even the familiar saying, 'money can't buy you class', or indeed *taste*, carried the suggestion that it really ought to; that disproportionate wealth was justified if the people profiting were able to demonstrate a certain style and flair.

For that reason, there will be two competing definitions of *taste* used throughout this book, hopefully expressed with enough clarity for it to be obvious which one I am using at any given time: the definition of taste that I would like for the world – related to quirks of personality and personal preference that have been allowed to evolve somewhat organically, and if not wholly individually, then at least without the tyranny of worrying about whether or not they might be 'right' or 'wrong'; and the definition that is commonly used today, and related to a sort of scoreboard of suitability and approval. From group to group, situation to situation, rules of taste will, of course, change. Yet often when I am referring to tastefulness throughout this book, I am referring to the standards upheld by the most powerful and influential, and therefore having the greatest impact on what we might term 'popular culture'. These are ideas of taste that most people living in Western societies will at least have some vague awareness of. But in addition to this, and with every observation I make, I want to encourage readers to also consider how this phenomenon plays out in even smaller dynamics; that regardless of the specific group or community judgement, it is also the severity of that judgement and its contribution to a sense of 'us versus them' that is most important and urgently requiring of our attention.

Scam or be scammed

Finally, the one additional and technical dimension to this discussion that must be covered before we are permitted to roam freely through the bizarre and often ridiculous world of tastefulness and all that it implies, is the downward social mobility that has been observed in the early stages of the twenty-first century. Younger generations have understandably leant on matters of taste and erudition, afforded by the opening up of university education, as a means of distinguishing themselves, and denigrating older generations whose wealth is hoarded through property.

Deployed successfully, it can lead to an entity that looms large in the public imagination, the scammer, whose most famous example is Anna Delvey, or as she was formerly known, Anna Sorokin – an icon to a generation, and the face that launched a thousand op-eds and podcast episodes. The 'fake heiress' of Manhattan, Delvey's enormous celebrity was born of an ability to exploit old systems of wealth, and circumnavigate economic exclusion, through little more than a manipulation of her image and style, and by harnessing people's manic fixation with taste. But more on Delvey later.

With all caveats, qualifications, disclaimers and definitions covered, it requires me only to say, then, that this is a book that considers the emerging industries of taste and the sticky and unsettling ways in which a fixation with taste impacts our lives, written by someone who has often felt the harsh judgement of others with respect to what she liked and did not like. I believe that fear of judgement is a condition of working-class life, created through a necessity of survival, and that much of the pop psychology regarding confidence fails to acknowledge that being impervious to the judgement of other people is a luxury of knowing that you are not dependent on it for survival. That said, the ways that people are made to feel maligned and undervalued in a system of degrading capitalism has allowed right-wing despots to seize certain visual codes and styles to their advantage, and only by understanding how they did this are we able to mount a serious and lasting challenge to the threat that they pose. Through a lot of personal reflection facilitated by the National Health Service and beyond, my relationship to that question of taste has now become slightly easier to contend with, and I enjoy a clarity of mind with respect to it that eluded me for many years. Having found it, I feel almost duty-bound to share with you what I have learned.

Chapter Two

Homes

Only the useful or the beautiful,	or	That which 'sparks joy'
WILLIAM MORRIS		MARIE KONDO

While writing this book I spent a period of time in Antwerp, Belgium, a city of immense wealth that is showcased in its famous and imposing multi-storey train station, as well as the old Flemish-style merchant houses that line the main square of Grote Markt. Antwerp is a central conduit of the global diamond trade, owing to Belgium's colonisation of what is now the Democratic Republic of Congo, and one of the richest sources of diamonds anywhere in the world. Despite that campaign forming one of the bloodiest and most brutal in European colonial history, not to mention a cause of natural resources continuing to be extracted from sub-Saharan Africa, the city's diamond business experiences no shame, advertising itself confidently in regular billboards, street signs, shop windows and guided tours dedicated to the subject.

As convenient entry points to the rest of Europe, Belgium and the Netherlands have historically harnessed the riches obtained by their merchant trading abilities to fund various forms of creativity that would help to assert the cultural dominance of the northern continent over the rest of the world. It was in Antwerp that the Flemish Renaissance of the sixteenth century was centred, the austere counterpoint to that which took place around the same time in Italy. This is where the visual language was fomented that we associate with Puritanism, the branch of Christianity pioneered by the Calvinists and which became the dominant doctrine in Flanders and several nearby countries. Its effects can still be felt today, as Antwerp continues to export to the rest of the world a mode of taste that favours the minimal and the faintly ironical. The Antwerp Six, including Dries Van Noten, were a set of influential fashion designers who graduated from the city's Royal Academy of Fine Arts during the 1980s. Along with another of the city's famous fashion designers, Martin Margiela, they cemented its modern reputation as a place of creative activity.

I was more interested, however, in the city's relationship with the built environment and interior design. I therefore made a visit to the southern suburb of Wijnegen, and a large gallery complex created by the interior designer and author Axel Vervoordt. Kanaal, as the name suggests, sits on the banks of one of the man-made waterways running south-west of the city and comprises several industrial spaces, including a series of looming former grain silos and ware-houses, that have been adapted into exhibition spaces or immersive installations. One can find here works by some of the most famous names in art, including James Turrell and Anish Kapoor, although in every case artists seem to have been chosen for their adherence to, or else commissioned to fulfil, Vervoordt's primary fixations with solemnity, harmony and a rejection of the more conspicuously commercial aspects of modern life (overlooking the reality of course, that despite whatever subdued output, these are some of the more commercially minded artists working today). It is this approach that underscores a design practice that has won Vervoordt global fame, and led to a signature brand of rustic minimalism that is often described through the principle of *wabi sabi*, a Japanese term referring to a 'natural simplicity' that favours organic approaches and the slight oddities that occur therein. In Vervoordt's case, the principle has been used to create uncluttered spaces of a loamy palette – terracottas, browns and creams – driftwood furniture, untreated walls (or at least having the appearance of being untreated), choice decorations in the form of artfully placed twigs, and low lighting.

What compelled me to take the bus from Antwerp city centre, along a series of nondescript roads into Belgian suburbia, was an interest in Vervoordt's status as a high priest of good taste, as well as his popularity among the rich and powerful. Since the 1990s, Vervoordt has attracted high-profile clients including Bill Gates and Bruce Willis, both of whom commissioned him to design their houses. But for younger generations, Vervoordt is perhaps best known as the man behind the home of Kim Kardashian and Kanye West: a vast, minimalist mansion in the exclusive neighbourhood of Calabasas in Greater Los Angeles, and the third character in one of the most widely publicised and controversial of celebrity divorces.

Reputedly costing \$60 million to renovate over six years, the house, which the couple only occupied together for a year before Kardashian filed for divorce, has been more widely documented than any other of Vervoordt's projects, owing to the couple's propensity for self-promotion and their use of social media. As such, its oddities have attracted a great deal of attention. The walls and furniture are exclusively off-white, while the sinks in the bathroom appear to be completely flat, as opposed to conical-shaped, a trick of design concealing the mechanisms of their drainage system. The centrepiece of the house however is a hallway resembling one of the perspective paintings of vast cathedrals by the Dutch Renaissance artist Pieter Saenredam. This space, which is favoured by Kardashian as the backdrop to her many at-home fashion shoots, inspired a popular impression of the house as being austere to the point of sinister, a succession of smooth, four-centred arches creating what is certainly an arresting, if not a particularly homely, spectacle.

In *The Edifice Complex: How the Rich and Powerful Shape the World* (2005), the design critic and curator Deyan Sudjic chronicles the ways in which political leaders and aspirants use architecture as part of their regimes to inspire awe, compound national identity and create hopeful visions of the future. By his estimation, 'Architecture feeds the egos of the susceptible. They grow more and more dependent on it to the point where architecture becomes an end in itself, seducing its addicts as they build more and more on an ever-larger scale.' Sudjic's focus is on the dictators and despots throughout history who have built awe-inspiring monuments to overwhelm and cajole the masses, including Hitler's plans for the Volkshalle, a vast dome-shaped structure that would have been situated in the centre of Berlin, Stalin's Hotel Ukraina and several other gargantuan structures in the centre of Moscow, the minimalist monuments constructed by Mussolini in Italy and those too ordered by the former first lady of the Philippines, Imelda Marcos. But the principle applies equally to businessmen and celebrities of the Western world, who enjoy a similar level of public influence if not direct political power – and are increasingly able to assert this through the virtual terrain of social media. This was not Kanye West's only foray into the built environment, after all. Before announcing plans to run in the 2020 presidential race, he also commissioned the construction of a series of prototypes for what he dubbed 'Yeezy Homes', inspired by the nomadic igloo-type houses favoured by the counterculture movements that had emerged on the West Coast of America during the 1960s, including the designs of the Ant Farm collective and Buckminster Fuller. In 2018 he also donated $10 million to James Turrell's Roden Crater project, in which the artist plans to hollow out and transform a giant volcanic cinder cone in the Painted Desert region of Northern Arizona. West's political ambitions are not mentioned here with any seriousness (his 2020 campaign, if it can be called that, was half-baked and disorganised – he only appeared on the ballots in eighteen states thanks to missing deadlines and would therefore never have won), but even as an aspiring leader of the free world, his personal residence provides a fascinating counterpoint to the design sensibility of the incumbent, and West's one-time friend, Donald Trump.

During the 2016 US election race, images began to circulate of Trump at home, credited to photographer Regine Mahaux and taken in 2010. In these photographs, Trump is captured alongside his wife Melania and youngest son Barron, who plays variously with a life-size cuddly lion (easily mistaken for the real thing at first glance), a set of toy cars and trucks. The home is a palatial suite that overlooks several other skyscrapers of Midtown Manhattan. The convivial family scene, however, is rendered somewhat jarring by the marble walls, gilded cornices, thrones, frescos, Greco-Roman urns and gleaming chandeliers that would allow the apartment to easily pass for the home of a villain in a Brian De Palma film. It had been largely designed by Henry Conversano, who was best known for working on casinos and whose list of clients, quite different to Vervoordt's, included Stephen Winn and Hugh Hefner.[1] What he had created was something like the neo-neo-classical terrain of the Ceausescu palace in Romania; Versailles on synthetic creatine, where excess and extravagance had themselves been cannibalised by the need to simply replicate, multiply, expand and engulf.

The right to space

Though it is not clear when the current interior design scheme of the Trump Tower apartment was first adopted, Trump Tower itself was built in 1983, in the era in which Trump's personal style seems to have been cemented, from his hair down to his mode of dress. Though neither West nor

Trump might be considered typical of the age in which he rose to fame, the wildly divergent approach that each took to achieving the same ends – namely, of creating a spectacle that each hoped would impress and inspire awe among the wider public, from the apartment in New York, to the faux Spartan proportions of the Vervoordt mansion in Calabasas – seemed to be a story about the visual language of power and how it had changed in the West over the past forty years.

To understand this better, and to sample for myself the work of a man identified as a figurehead of a popular new minimalism, I battled the strong winds for which the Belgian lowlands are famous, making my way from the bus stop and along a series of pedestrianised A-roads. By the time I arrived, I was wet and dishevelled and was met with a look of derision that I have come to expect from people working in the design profession, from the woman who was sat behind the counter. She scanned my outfit before offering me a partial and somewhat curious smile and then handed me a map and a fob in the shape of a pebble and explained that I would need to raise it to the circular nodes that could be found at intervals around the space.

This required me to follow a sparse map that directed me along several paths that led to different buildings. I am not a cynic, and it would have been quite easy for me to approach this experience with the withering outlook of so many journalists looking to score a quick point against rarefied forms of expression that they do not immediately understand, but spending several hours lost among the different sites, bleeping my way into large hallways whose purpose was not always clear, but which in every case instilled in me a sense of serenity, was to understand Vervoordt's appeal. In a world where almost every experience is optimised for profit and consumer engagement, it is rare to simply wander aimlessly through different buildings, with little expectation of what might lurk behind each door. It lacks the signage and instructive layout of most contemporary art galleries. Compared with the maddening bureaucracy and garish advertising of the world outside, Kanaal is a place of escape, whose views, proportions and function have all been factored into the design, which allows you ascend large staircases made of a russet oxidised steel, and reach square windows framing scenes of still ponds containing bulrushes and lily pads. In an otherwise empty room, a solitary, bow-shaped rod hangs from the ceiling, creating the appearance of a thin incision having been made to the space, and like the slashed canvasses of the celebrated Italian postmodernist, Lucio Fontana. In another room, large concrete balls stand among pillars in a former warehouse, disturbing an otherwise angular space. Tuning out from everything but the basic sensations of tactility, shape and form is gratifying.

Before leaving, I followed the path to a final installation situated at the perimeter, created by James Turrell. This secular chapel allowed only the scarcest amount of light, such that, and despite written assurances that I should be able to find my way around, I was forced to run a finger along its curved wall as I made my way into a hallway that I could only grasp after my eyes had adjusted – a process that took several minutes, after which a dim square of light was revealed on the opposite wall. I spent perhaps half an hour there in total, my mind eventually emptying of thoughts and experiencing a serenity that is maybe only possible through sensory deprivation.

I left with a feeling of weightlessness, making my way out of the compound and back towards the bus stop. But as we trundled along the same roads back to Antwerp, I noticed this time how many interior design and furniture stores lined the route. Here we were met with the financial realities of trying to recreate the Vervoordt experience at home – or the transformation of the Vervoordt approach into a lifestyle that might be sold to the masses – with stores peddling flimsy versions of minimal design objects, including variations on the Flos Arco floor lamp and the Mies van der Rohe Barcelona Chair. My serenity soon disappeared, as we glided past store after store containing items stacked high and carelessly alongside variously coloured shag rugs, sequin wall hangings and novelty clocks. To recreate even a fraction of the same serenity within the average home would be impossible, and I was struck by how much wealth is required in the occlusion of outside noise, certainly under the present conditions of capitalism in which billions of us are forced to work longer hours and often across multiple jobs. Reduced to *objet* – that is, decorative stuff – the idea of the Vervoordt project, and minimalism more broadly, ceases to work. Perhaps it is only Bill Gates and Bruce Willis who currently possess the means with which to do it justice.

In her memoir *The Lonely City* (2016), Olivia Laing asks whether hoarding isn't a class-based judgement. After all, owning lots of stuff is only ever a problem for those who are short on space, and storage. About the photographer Vivian Maier, whose large collection of personal belongings have been cited as evidence of a dysfunction, Laing writes, 'All these people talk about her hoarding, the pack-rat way she went through life. Watching, I couldn't help but feel their reactions were at least partly about money and social status; about who has the right to ownership and what happens when people exceed the number of possessions that their circumstance and standing would ordinarily allow.' Hoarding is almost never considered a dysfunction in the wealthy with their sprawling homes – the notion almost ceases to exist once you enter that world. It seemed possible, then, that sparsity, and a lack of clutter, had become the fixation of generation endemically short on space, owing to widespread housing shortages and soaring rents; and that this was now the fashionable mode adopted even by that generation's wealthy celebrities and public figures who could afford large homes.

The rise in popularity of websites celebrating sparse, mid-century design, such as The Modern House, a British estate agent and online lifestyle magazine founded in 2005 that specialises in design-led properties, would certainly seem to suggest that a virtue had been made of emptiness. By the mid-2010s, this authority on matters of domestic charm had achieved cult-like following, with thousands of subscribers and daily readers. Scrolling through the images on its site, of homes that are stripped back, airy but hardly appearing to be very lived in, it is easy to see how a generation of renters forced into house shares due to soaring house prices, for example, might have projected fantasies of a life unencumbered by drudgery, or stuff. But in combining an e-commerce and editorial function, the site also aided the perception, one that had started decades previously with the selling off of social housing, of homes as objects of consumer desire, rather than a necessity and a human right. Estate agents had been doing this for years, of course, only now with the lifestyle magazine and site of purchase located in the same place, it became increasingly difficult to discern vested interest from reportage. More importantly, by virtue of having fulfilled aesthetic standards that were in part being set by The Modern House, homes sold on its website were listed at a higher price than otherwise, and in this way it contributed to the very problem from which many people were using it as a form of virtual escape.

Grey matter

If an abundance of free space was the goal, or at least the appearance of free space, then it would also explain the rise in demand for homes that were dark and imposing – in what might at first sound like a paradox to the demand for minimalism and the look popularised by The Modern House and sites like it. What began in fashionable urban enclaves soon found its way into the luxury spaces, as well as the suburban mainstream, so that by the year 2020, a representative from the architectural paint retailer Dulux told me that the company had seen a four-fold increase in the sale of grey paint over the previous five years. If the conventional wisdom – which was always held as true and incontestable – maintained that magnolia and white were optimal choices of colour, allowing spaces to appear larger and more breezy, then this was also only relevant in providing satisfaction to the people who lived there. If impressions and cultural capital were more important than personal pleasure, and if we had increasingly started to think of our homes through the limited view of a snapshot that might be shared with the outside world, then darker colours would signal abundance: of a home so rich in space as to forgo optical illusions and tricks of the light that might enlarge and expand it. Not just that, but to rent, after all, was to live in sterile boxes, kitted out to the minimum standard with cheap, plastic mod cons – known colloquially as 'white goods' – by landlords eager to maximise their return on investment. To rent was to be prevented from decorating and to keep one's living space as unencumbered as possible for the sake of attracting the next round of tenants. If white and magnolia were, for the aspirant middle and lower classes, the colours of transience, then grey and similar shades, in many cases denoted *ownership*; an indication to friends, neighbours and a cohort of online followers of your arrival on the market.

But there was something else at play too in the houses, coffee shops and fashion stores of Western Europe and North America turning dark, as we awoke in the mid-2010s to find that the walls, window frames and kitchen units of these private residences and consumer establishments had become thick with a layer of industrial soot. The sixty-watt tungsten glow and stainless-steel sheen of the exuberant 1990s and 2000s had gone, and what stood in its place was a burning gold filament lamp, chlorophyll-rich foliage, copper pots and light-absorbent flagstone floors. This Dickensian colour palette was everywhere, as millions of people painted their homes, or at least certain aspects of them, charcoal, indigo or slate. The streets of Bushwick and Williamsburg in Brooklyn, Echo Park and Silver Lake in Los Angeles, Dalston and Stoke Newington in London, the 10th and 11th Arrondissements in Paris, and the Jordaan in Amsterdam, had all been transformed into theme parks of a bygone bliss known only to the cast and crew of TV period dramas. To walk down these streets was to experience life in desaturation, a monochromatic filter having been applied over every scene, complete with market-goers in distressed blue-collar worker jackets and twill cotton slacks.

How had the Brooklyn of the nineteenth century found its way into the Brooklyn of the present day – and beyond that too, into the wealthier neighbourhoods of the Upper East Side? Darker colours, after all, would have been favoured by the original occupants of the former industrial tenements and terrace houses that were now being bought up by corporate professionals. Because if white had been the colour of wealthy palaces and townhouses two centuries earlier, or at least their fixtures – belonging to families who had the means of renewing it with fresh coats of paint and regular cleans, not to mention being closeted from the fumes and the gathering soot of impoverished slums – then dark colours were naturally favoured by those poorer urban communities.

But revivalism alone would be too simplistic, as is the explanation about ownership. If history really was a factor, then the response was surely disingenuous by virtue of being purely aesthetic. After all, these neighbourhoods in which the trend first emerged were no longer slums, but fast becoming some of the wealthiest areas in the Western world. To reflect the reality of life in the nineteenth century would have required them to carry the high gloss sheen of affluence, demonstrating the gilded riches that were now presided over by a new type of yuppie.

A more likely explanation is that these neighbourhoods

were associated with, and even became shorthand for, a very particular corporate-professional type and new economic entity: the 'creative'. Since the mid-2000s, *creativity*, the word, had been stretched to absolute breaking point, encompassing everything from cross-stitch to algorithmic coding for artificial intelligence. In reality, the 'creative industries' referred to anything that relied on print and digital media, and the myriad forms that the latter now took: advertising, PR, social media management, music management, content creation, producing, publishing, coding, e-commerce, marketing and designing. According to official figures published by the government in 2019, the so-called creative industries accounted for 3.2m or 9.6 per cent of all UK jobs.[2] To be clear, when I refer to the 'creative' throughout this book, I am not referring to the artist, the writer or the journalist – practitioners who resist and challenge the work of the advertising industry, and who should reject their verbal categorisation alongside it.

These industries – various in type but mostly connected in their reliance on the internet and digital technology – were somewhat resistant to the storm of the 2008 financial crisis. By 2020, they were reputed to be growing five times faster than the UK economy, and contributing £13 million to it per hour.

Setting aside the fact that by today's logic, the question seems less to be *what constitutes a creative career?*, and more like *what can feasibly be categorised under the rubric of creativity in order to make it sound more appealing?*, for all these reasons, the new yuppie no longer thought of himself as a corporate type in a suit and tie. Instead, he enjoyed wealth, while maintaining the delusion of his moral and creative integrity. His bank balance might resemble the trader of yesteryear, but his clothes would be far closer to that of a beatnik; his healthcare plan might be premium, but his home decor would have the look and feel of a consumptive chimney sweep. This wealth was still largely being accumulated among the older, more established members of these booming industries, while younger entrants who were actually generating most of that wealth would also bear the brunt of more lax employment protocols that the 'creative' moniker allowed for: short-term contracts, rolling 'permalance' exploitation, payment through perks.

The conventional bourgeois trappings of the business class would not fly with the senior creative ad person, for whom charcoal paint, not to mention the revived interest in cotton twill, farmers markets and produce, would help to satisfy a sense of artistic integrity. In his stand-out 1979 work *Distinction*, on the cultural preferences of Right- and Left-Bank residents in Paris, Pierre Bourdieu found that while those who had made their wealth through business and entrepreneurialism tended to be *bon vivants* and drawn to more joyful, bright and sparkly expressions of wealth and status – delicate, exquisite meals, musical ensembles of the Viennese Court and the paintings of Wattau and Renoir – those members of the bourgeoisie whose status had been acquired through education, per *Frasier*, favoured more simple, rustic items – antique shops, second-hand 'finds', 'simple' clothes, the paintings of Goya and the music of Sebastian Bach.[3] What we were witnessing then, in the dark wainscoting of Soho House, and the timberwork of every grain store and independent brewery, was perhaps something like the conflation of these two groups, and the hope of many in being able to defy the imperatives of the market economy and combine the prestige of the auteur with the paygrade of a chartered surveyor.

The existence of this new economic group would be down to the rapid expansion in communications technology that happened to also coincide with the financial crash. This technology would not only create new jobs that were visual by nature – in most cases producing goods that were disseminated via screen – but would itself play a part in shaping aesthetic standards due to the highly addictive reward mechanisms of its creation. The home improvement shows of the 1990s had been usurped by Instagram and Pinterest, whose *like* and *share* functions would dictate a culture of conformity and replication. At the same time, too, this faux austerity of the kind found in the more pared-back, crude and homespun fashions of a world post-2008, conveniently served as a foil for a society whose inequalities were still stubbornly entrenched. Beloved of the aspirant middle classes, it nevertheless painted a world of rustic proportions whose outward appearance would seem to be more equal and open than ever before. Gone were the flashy displays of wealth, creating a semblance of what we have already established the Conservative Party in power liked to claim was now a 'classless' society (this was the term used by John Major in 1990, to describe his immediate ambitions for the UK).

By the time I started renting for myself, homes had also become an extension of the tradable identity, and were arranged accordingly and for optimal online shareability, giving rise to the trend for interiors blogs centred on desk spaces with artfully arranged stationery and notice boards, stacks of books and various house plants; sparse minimalism colliding with a degree of 'curated' clutter. There were degrees to this, of course. For the wealthy, it was abundant; for the younger and hard up, more elliptical, with the tendency mentioned previously of trying to create small vignettes of respectability in the shabby corners of rented bedrooms. This was roundly mocked by an older generation, keen to denounce those younger than it as recklessly indulgent, wasting their would-be house deposits on coffee shop coffees, avocado toasts and candles. Without even going into how trite and overplayed this false observation has become, not to mention the absurd economics of the complaint, it seems necessary to stress the glaring misapprehension that this was in any way a reflection of excess, rather than its opposite. The transformation of such basic sustenance as a *coffee* or a *slice of grilled bread* or *a piece of paper with words on it* into objects of desirability, such that people felt compelled to post about them online, is possibly the most vivid expression of the crisis faced by a generation. It is nothing if not sad that they staked their place in luxury through the sharing of a bowl of picante olives.

For the downwardly mobile generation (relative to its parents) for whom salvation and status could only be sought in the realm of the virtual and the visual, interiors manuals were nevertheless obliging, and catered to both the more illustrious and the hard up. This accounts for the popularity of magazines such as *The Modern House*, but also *The Selby*, *Apartmento*, and *Apartment Therapy*, which established their popularity through an emphasis on *economy*, or at least its appearance. These were magazines that focused on the art of thrifting, upcycling, customising and adapting. Their popularity stemmed from a generation forced to contend with confined living spaces, becoming increasingly resourceful with their one-bedroom kingdoms whose proportions could be partially concealed or exaggerated through the careful crop of a single image. In the 'shelfie' that was popularised around this time too – a feature used by magazines to showcase the personality of whichever influencer or celebrity was being profiled, and consisting of the subject discussing the various objects of note *that had shaped the person they are today* – one publication cropped up more than most.

Bibles of taste

Kinfolk first appeared on shelves in 2011, and over the following decade came to represent the high watermark of an aesthetic that defined middlebrow good taste – an analogue reality comprising objects of a pastoral idyll and a mid-century modernist utopia. Despite being based in Copenhagen, and exporting an idea of Scandinavian design, *Kinfolk* was the creation of four North American friends who first met while studying at the Brigham Young University campus in Hawaii. The magazine's first home was the city of Portland, Oregon, and the most famous of its four founders, Nathan Williams – the 'face' of the brand, if you like – began his career as an analyst at Goldman Sachs.

Williams only left his job in banking as the magazine began to accrue its vast readership. By 2016, *Kinfolk* reported circulation figures of 80,000, 70 per cent of which it claimed consisted of people working in or around the so-called 'creative industries'. Launching just nine months after the creation of Instagram, *Kinfolk* quickly started to dictate the Kodak-filtered aesthetic of the platform's lifestyle bloggers. In the late 2010s, few new online brands existed whose visual style wasn't in some way indebted to *Kinfolk*'s idealistic depiction of craft and artisanal methods, natural produce, natural-dyed clothing and soft furnishings, sparsity and simultaneous eclecticism.

In many ways, *Kinfolk*'s aesthetic represented a modern take on that which was peddled by a much earlier magazine and discussed by Bourdieu, *Connaissance de la Campagne*.[4] This mid-century French interiors and lifestyle guide, which Bourdieu discusses for its tendency of 'appropriating "nature" – birds, flowers, landscapes', peddled an albeit more rural, slightly more conservative lifestyle that was never-theless similar to *Kinfolk* for its emphasis on simplicity and slowing down. The magazine, he argued, 'presupposes a cul-ture, the privilege of those who have ancient roots. Owning a chateau, a manor house or grange is not only a question of money; one must also appropriate it, appropriate the cellar and learn the art of bottling, described as "an act of deep communion with the wine" which every "believer" should have performed "at least once", acquire trophies, the secrets of fishing, the skills of gardening, competences which are both ancient and slowly learned, like cooking or the knowledge of wines; appropriate, in a word, the art of living of the aristo-crat, or country gentleman, indifferent to the passage of time and rooted in things which last.'[5]

Connaissance de la Campagne, and publications like it,

emphasised the value of leisureliness and tradition. The most desirable homes were those that carried the markings of lineage, be that through age, or through their inclusion of old heirlooms and creations that were the product of long-held family recipes or techniques. But as the author Lynsey Hanley has pointed out in her book on the subject of class, social-mobility and manners, *Respectable: Crossing the Class Divide* (2017), the traditions in question must necessarily favour the upper classes, due to the practical impediments that working people face in being able to preserve any kind of connection from generation to generation. Not only does the necessity of hard work mean that most people have little time to maintain practical traditions, but the mechanisms of cultural conservation have also been decimated for people who have been encouraged to feel shame towards themselves and their backgrounds – who in order to *pull themselves up*, must feel suspicion and distrust towards the friends and family that would otherwise serve as the basis of a secure and solid identity. '[Some] see this profound loss as a family legacy whose continued transmission they must break for the sake of their own children,' writes Hanley, of the rules imposed by a system of social mobility. 'To do the latter may require leaving – physically and socially, if not emotionally – the environment in which your character was formed. In so doing, you risk creating another disjuncture, another source of loss, in the history of your family. The place you came from, so this new story goes, wasn't good enough for you [...] The difficulty comes when you have a thought that goes along the lines of "I believe life can be better than this"; a thought which is then interpreted by other people as "You believe you're better than me."'[6]

The crafts that are revered and passed down by these publications then – crochet, needlecraft, clothes-making, pottery, preserving – are often only able to be carried down between generations of one particular demographic, and their value is therefore tied up in the tacit communication of a proximity to wealth and status, as well as the conveyance of free leisure time. This could be primary or secondary: one's own ability to cultivate and perfect a given craft, or the ability to afford items that have been handmade by others. In both cases the same principle applies: in yearning for goods that are, or at least have the appearance of being, homespun and handmade, a sense of distinction is derived from the vast amount of time devoted to their creation, be that in the immediate sense of how long it has taken them to be made, or in the sense of being the product of several generation's worth of wisdom. It is specifically the machine-made quality of those products that furnish the homes of so many people on earth, who do not have the means nor the time to adjust their consumption habits, that lends the hand-crafted its superior market value and desirability.

This might be obvious, but it is worth pointing out. If distinction is always predicated on being able to afford the scarcest and therefore most sought-after commodities, then the surplus models that define the present era of capitalism have made a luxury of time: time-honoured traditions, handmade laboriously wrought pots and objects that require us to 'slow down' in order to make use of them. Terrariums, planters, at-home sourdough starter kits all command a retail price disproportionate to their practical utility as a result, and despite 'utility' being the primary focus of their branding.

But as with everything under capitalism, even that imperviousness to the stress and strain of daily life, and the slow evolution and preservation of tradition that underscores the design sensibility celebrated by someone like Axel Vervoordt, and in magazines such as *Kinfolk*, may also be artificially replicated, simulated or made virtual. This leads us to the unusual story of Gin Lane, the creative agency founded by entrepreneur Emmett Shine and responsible for some of the most popular brands of the 2010s, including fashion retailer Everlane, shaving retailer Harry's, and salad bar Sweetgreen – companies primed for success with a design sensibility that was straight from the *Kinfolk* playbook. With muted colours, utilitarian typefaces and natural photography, each was able to give a modern twist to the cotton slack (Everlane), everyday shaver (Harry's) and humble lunchtime salad (Sweetgreen).

Yet despite having made his (somewhat improbable) name in this way, Gin Lane founder Shine announced in 2019 that he would soon be changing focus. In response to what he termed 'burnout culture', Shine decided to apply his skills and the purview of his creative agency to *life itself*, the one thing that had yet to be rebranded in its entirety. The result was Pattern, a company of vague parameters, promising to deliver at one time or another, products and services ranging from talks on the benefits of mindfulness, to chunky kitchen utensils, trivets and desktop storage solutions. The brand's website contains an invite to 'join its family', and in an earlier iteration contained a painterly masthead depicting bucolic scenes of a meadow, mountains, a cottage and a peach tree, above which reads the line: 'Pattern is a family of brands designed to help you enjoy daily life.' These brands include

Open Spaces, selling a range of home storage solutions whose name uses the terminology of the common land; Letterfolk, selling various toys and home accessories, including 'hand crafted letter boards' and 'nostalgic clocks', which, according to the bio on its Instagram page, have been 'inspired by simpler times'; and Yield, a 'housewares' and 'apothecary' retailer harnessing the language of agriculture. Visitors to the Pattern site can choose to browse by product or Persona, the latter of which includes 'The Organiser', 'The Artist', 'The Home Chef' and, you guessed it, 'The Curator'. As journalist Anne Helen Petersen highlighted, Pattern exemplified the level of doublethink involved in so much modern branding, its express purpose being to assist people in getting beyond the artifice of advertising and modern consumerism. As she puts it, Pattern was 'a brand, with $14 million in venture capital behind it, to fix what brands hath wrought'.[7]

This brings us back to our friend Nathan Williams, who after many years of working at *Kinfolk*, took a step back to lead the creative agency attendant to the Canadian bookstore chain, Indigo. Much like the statements on the Pattern website, the Instagram bio for Indigo states that it is 'Canada's largest purveyor of ideas and inspiration to enrich your life #yourhappyplace', beneath which are numerous posts containing images of seascapes, beds situated in forests, fireplaces and artfully arranged food spreads. As if our mother's first function had been to sell us beauty products via makeup tutorials, one caption describes her as: 'Mom the first, Mom the friend, Mom – your original influencer'. During an interview with *Vanity Fair* in 2020, Williams described his role at Indigo and how the experience at *Kinfolk* had helped him, summoning a hollow corporate pastoralism that seemed to finally complete the link between the aesthetic of the magazine and its role in concealing the objectives of commerce: 'We've been doing focus groups, asking our customers, what are your pain points. And they are exactly the ones we were addressing at *Kinfolk*. People say, "I'm so connected digitally but I feel a total lack of real connection. How do I find the balance? How do I find a community?"'[8] The logic prior to the expansion of this corporate pastoralism would have been to forego social media altogether, perhaps earn less and disengage from most forms of modern advertising. But as we were starting to move beyond that, the creative agencies exemplified here, and their attendant magazines, were instead creating a virtual serenity, one that would be achieved through shopping experiences and online talks, whose entry fee would be paid almost automatically and without hesitation, so desperate were we to remedy the stresses that they were drumming up elsewhere within the screen.

The doyen of millennial chic had finally made explicit what we knew all along: that balance, community and utility were being used to serve the ends of capital. If the opposite of work and commerce – rest, relaxation and disengagement from capitalism – could be simulated and sold back to us, then there was no escape from the reality of commerce and advertising. As Debord writes, '... imprisoned in a flattened universe, bound by the screen of the spectacle behind which his life has been deported, [the spectator] knows only the fictional speakers who unilaterally surround him with their commodities and the politics of their commodities.'[9]

The wholesale absorption of reality into this language of

visual marketing now complete, a new world existed, whose every harm could also be solved by some additional product, service or talk. As a result, there would appear to be no morality outside of consumerism. Each person would be reduced to their spending habits, paving the way for a situation that made a hallowed figure of the arcane and knowing consumer, and a miscreant of those forced to buy cheap and to buy fast.

Baroque tactics

When we consider minimalism of a type described here, but difficult to recreate in practise, its opposite is not just mass-produced tat, but also gilded riches. The Baroque refers to a distinct moment in art history that followed the Dutch and Italian Renaissance and Mannerism periods in art, but more colloquially, it has also come to mean that which is excessive and gaudy. Consider *The Queen of Versailles* (2012), a documentary by Lauren Greenfield, which tells the story of how timeshare magnate David Siegel and his wife Jackie embarked on a highly ambitious, and blighted, endeavour to build one of America's largest homes. The House of Versailles was meant to be partially inspired by the French palace of the same name, albeit this time in Orange County, Florida. It is a story of idiocy and excess that demonstrates just how untethered from logic and sound reason the capitalist imaginary of America had become, as the Siegels sank almost everything they had into a 90,000-square-foot building of cartoonish proportions, while Siegel's businesses became embattled by the US recession. Watching their story unfold feels emblematic, as if we are witnessing the final fulfilment of Sudjic's comment in action, of architecture 'seducing its addicts as they build more and more on an ever larger scale' – the ultimate capitulation of wealth to *bigness*.

But part of what makes the spectacle of the Siegels so entertaining is just how elementary and out of time it also feels. Society has a tendency to forgive extreme wealth when its psychological trappings are a little more sophisticated and complex. How many times have you had to sit through some bore telling you that Warren Buffett lives in a modestly sized house, for example, as if modest tastes could absolve someone of their place in an exploitative class system? By contrast, of course, Trump's home was roundly mocked by the commentariat. As Peter York wrote for *Politico*: ' . . . these homes don't exist to express personal collecting passions or evolved tastes. ('If a reason to invade Iraq was wanted,' the American political satirist P.J. O'Rourke once wrote, describing Saddam's chandeliers, 'felony interior decorating would have done.') Dictators can't understand why anyone would go for the genially scaled-back charm of Western Old Money houses in Cambridge, England, or Cambridge, Massachusetts. Why have old when you can have new, matte when you can have shiny, small when you can have huge? There is no subtlety or understatement, let alone irony.'[10]

What this assessment fails to recognise, however, is that regardless of whether Trump himself computed such irony, images have a way of existing beyond their creator. Trump's home, along with his entire media presence, was inflected with an irony that unfortunately only endeared him to voters. It also ignored the fact that the Baroque carried a potent subtext that needn't be understood intellectually to be understood implicitly, thanks to what it has come to represent over so many centuries. Marking a point of departure between classical convention in art in an era of global capitalism, it is an aesthetic that contains a clear rejection of inherited wisdom, tutelage and posterity – first promoted by the Catholic Church, it was quickly adopted by the aristocracy and ascendant, merchant classes of Europe who were profiting from the spoils of colonialism, who in a bid to demonstrate their wealth, would go to ever-more extreme lengths in terms of the size and complexity of the buildings, sculptures and paintings they commissioned. Prior to its emergence, and famously in the traditions of the Flemish and Italian Renaissance, art favoured and supported by the European aristocracy had been predicated on the idea of mastery – long artistic dynasties forged in a small number of prized studios and ateliers, generations of wisdom being handed down through a carefully protected system of schooling. The Baroque, by contrast, and certainly the Late Baroque and Rococo, was often the expression of a newly created wealth that disdained the protected avenues of high culture and its teaching, tearing up the rule book and dictating that art and creative expression be freed of any prior rules and constraints. The capitalist class, who were not necessarily well educated or well versed in the ways of fine art, identified a tyranny in the patronage of the arts and the standards that it upheld (without realising, or perhaps just flagrantly ignoring, the tyranny that they presented to millions of subjugated people worldwide).

It is little surprise, then, that the Baroque aesthetic enjoyed something of a revival in British and American culture during the Thatcher and Reagan years of the 1980s and into the 1990s, representing as they did times of further economic liberalism. But that trend, and the Baroque more broadly, would also start to be satirised, through the wry output of brands such as Versace, that exaggerated the bright colours, gold details and Cartouche motifs of the style, as an ironic riposte to both the more traditional and socially conservative values of the church and the WASPy strains of culture that prevailed in American high society. One of the defining characteristics of Protestantism of course had been the humble rejection of Catholic excess. That relationship was complicated considerably, but not only, by the exportation of Protestantism, and particularly Presbyterianism, to North America in the seventeenth and eighteenth centuries, where it was practised by the elite.

As has already been covered, Bourdieu found that the *nouveau riche* and those made wealthy through business, commerce and entrepreneurialism in the twentieth century nevertheless still held a preference for the works of Watteau and Pierre-Auguste Renoir – the latter being an impressionist by proximity and some painterly approaches, but a baroque painter in spirit, much like Watteau, who revived, or perhaps helped to maintain, popular interest in romantic subject matter, florid detail and saccharine, over-saturated colours. In what therefore reads like a perfect fable of contemporary right-wing popularity, Trump had a *fake* Renoir hanging from the wall of his apartment. During an interview with Melania Trump conducted by journalist Greta Van Sustern for Fox News, but also featured in several news segments with various broadcasters, a gilt frame could be seen hanging from the walls of the Trump apartment and containing an image of two female figures, both in bonnets and cradling a basket of flowers, created with the same quivering brush strokes that gave them the quintessential Renoir haze and sun-dappled etherealness. In truth, the work was a replica of *Two Sisters on the Terrace* (1881), which had been kept at the Art Institute of Chicago since the mid-1930s. According to journalist Tim O'Brien, the replica had once hung from the interior of the businessman's private jet, where O'Brien claims that he had tried to persuade Trump of its obvious fakery, a suggestion that the would-be president at that point, rejected out of hand.

As Debord writes: 'The disappearance of historical art, which was linked to the internal communication of an elite and had its semi-independent social basis in the partly playful conditions still lived by the last aristocracies, also expresses the fact that capitalism possesses the first-class power which admits itself stripped of any ontological quality, a power which, rooted in the simple management of the economy, is equally the loss of all human mastery.'[11] If the baroque had begun life as a rejection of past tradition and as a celebration of unbridled excess – an aesthetic divorced from tradition or past ideological schema – then over time it had come to acquire the emblematic status of the cash-rich and the culturally bankrupt, of those scorned and derided by the cultural establishment, as they believed, and who, in an act of subversion, wielded that rejection as a point of pride. As such, this gilded, imperialist aesthetic had become shorthand for a type of withering irreverence; and partly also on account of the internet with its tendency to flatten everything to appearances, so that it became difficult to decipher between examples of straightforward excess, and the ways in which the baroque had been ironised and parodied. Dumb vulgarity then is too easy and inadequate an assessment.

Where Peter York was mistaken, and where commentators like him might have actually served to boost Trump's popularity, was in thinking that the dictator aesthetic, as he put it, was incidental to the dictator's success, as opposed to it being a cornerstone. For those who felt humiliated by a degrading class system and inequality, not to mention a currency of cultural capital that was reaching a level of cacophony, Trump's brazen and unapologetic wealth might have spelled rebellion, resistance and pride. Even without Trump knowing it, even without our conscious recognition of it, his aesthetic choices carried with them a very vivid set of signifiers. This is how, and somewhat paradoxically, the gilded hell-house became almost immune to criticism.

If Trump is the human embodiment of the rich and tasteless, then Boris Johnson makes a slight adjustment on that model by embodying the rich and the careless, where carelessness refers to both an apparently charming ineptitude and an imperviousness to the judgement of other people. Photos taken of the interior at 10 Downing Street, transformed with the loving care of Johnson's partner Carrie Johnson (née Symonds) into a coloniser's boudoir replete with safari tapestries and painted portraits of local subjects, would certainly support this latter definition. Where Johnson's preferred style, much like Princess Anne's living room, carried the emblems of inherited wealth with its much more antiquated and homely accessories than the Trumpian march of endless marble tabletops and gold finishes, then both nevertheless contained a rejection of the prim and conspicuously anxious aesthetics of the ascendent professional class.

If these houses didn't inspire horror in the minds of the electorate, then it was partly on account of how far the aspirational mode had shifted in favour of the stripped-back and the austere. It was our fixation with simplicity, ironically, that was undergoing a farcical cannibalisation at the hands of capitalism – that was being transformed in a baroque fashion into pastiche. In a world of human commodity value, where nothing is more dangerous or threatening to a low-income person's livelihood than the insinuation that they might be clueless, dumb or devoid of taste, and on account of forces described previously – the growing ubiquity of social media and a corporate emphasis on image and conformity – the popularity of these leaders starts to make more sense. Regardless of how brazen their displays of wealth might have been, in fact *because* of that very brazenness, or apparent cluelessness, they would seem to legitimise a crime that millions of other people in our image-obsessed society believed they stood accused of.

On the one hand then, we can see how the gaudy entrapments of Trump Tower, and to a lesser extent the Johnson refurbishment of 10 Downing Street, might not present the same egregious spectacle to everyone, and might even represent something more honest, straightforward and relatable than the pervasive modes of good taste found in the corporate-professional sphere. And not just because they serve as shorthand, necessarily, for the harmful beliefs and attitudes. The Kardashian-West house, with its chicness in overdrive, its understatedness on steroids, served as the more extreme example of a tendency that had been building for many years, and which, in its conspicuous denial of wealth and mass production, was also liable to accusations of hypocrisy.

Carmela's cabinet

Like so many issues that only became more apparent in the years after it first aired, the TV show *The Sopranos* provides us with a scene that perfectly encapsulates many of these ideas. Centred on the life of mafia boss Tony Soprano, the HBO drama series took an unorthodox approach to the gangland format by introducing the dimension of psychoanalysis. When Tony suffers panic attacks and seeks out the help of psychiatrist Dr Jennifer Melfi, a fascinating thesis begins to unfold on the subconscious urges of the modern man, the American citizen and the second-generation immigrant. Among other things, *The Sopranos* dealt in the criminal hypocrisy of America's banking sector and the violence contained within its image of the suburban idyll, as well as the vilification of immigrant communities with limited recourse to formal avenues of employment. For me, as I am sure is true for many viewers, the show is most illuminating in its domestic concerns, as main character Tony seeks to reconcile the bloody nature of his work with the respectable ambitions that he holds for his family. Wife Carmela, daughter Meadow and son Anthony Jr, hold a dysfunctional but in many ways accurate mirror to the values of American society, and across six seasons, their successes, failures, happinesses and sorrows, pose the question of what we are all willing to ignore, or disavow in ourselves, in order to achieve a level of financial comfort.

The scene in question occurs in an episode from the first season, 'A Hit is a Hit'– a double-entendre referring to both Tony's success in pulling off a recent heist, and scoring big on the golf course. In the episode, Tony is invited by his neighbour, and the family's doctor, Bruce Cusamano, to play a round of golf at the local members' club. Tony accepts the invite in the hope that it will allow him to mix with *meddigans* – an Italian-American term given to white Americans who are not of Italian descent – and ultimately learn something about playing the stock market. The episode, which elsewhere contains a rather more problematic storyline involving junior mobster Christopher Moltisanti and a gangster rapper, is nevertheless striking in its treatment of issues related to social standing and cultural capital. If taste is a tacit theme of the show, weaving its way in with distinctive fashions and interior design schemes – themselves now the subject of a million dedicated blogs and Instagram feeds – then in this episode, as with occasional others, it is also an explicit focus of the plot.

During their golfing trip, Cusamano's friends grill Tony on subjects ranging from *The Godfather* (1972) to Al Capone. It is not the interaction he had hoped for. Despite all of his bravado in response, confidence in Melfi later reveals a deeper hurt caused by this event, as does the episode's concluding scene in which Tony is seen lifting weights from his bench press and letting out a series of anguished sighs. We come to realise that Tony wants to be accepted by respectable America, and in many ways assimilate, in a theme that is expanded on in his interactions with his children: the precocious Meadow and the nihilistic Antony Jr, whose own intellectual and professional awakenings present their own set of existential challenges.

When Cusamano eventually and cowardly admits to Tony that he cannot make him a member of the club, it is not just as a result of Tony's profession, but, we suspect, his inability, or perhaps refusal, to acquiesce and appease the touristic lens of the established middle class.

Materially, Tony is no different to his new acquaintances, living in the same kind of neighbourhood and enjoying many of the same luxuries. What he lacks, of course, is cultural capital – or to use the vernacular of early 2000s New Jersey, carefully and with irony of course, what he lacks, is *class*. Tony Soprano might be an unlikely way in here, but his example serves to demonstrate that the cleft in meaning that the word 'class' had undergone reflected a complication in the dynamics of the real world, or at least in the real world of *The Sopranos*, where economic and social mobility did not always correspond. It also transformed the inequalities felt by immigrant communities in this instance, into a quirk of personality or character, and thereby also reinforced the *de facto* status of class hierarchies, and in so doing, also made an unquestionable marker of achievement and moral purity out of certain objects.

Before Tony's golf outing, Cusamano hosts a dinner party for several of his friends, including Dr Melfi. At one point in the evening the friends discuss the oddity of Tony's presence on an otherwise quiet and respectable street, and the possible effect on house prices. Cusamano fends off criticism for associating with Tony by claiming that there is little meaningful difference between gang activity and the unscrupulous practises enacted by the corporate financial sector. To which his female associates respond aghast in what seems a fairly accurate estimation of the hypocritical Christian conservative tendencies concentrated among white middle-class housewives. Following this, the friends discuss a recent fundraiser, held in the Sopranos' back garden, where a lack of guns and conspicuous violence had surprised them all. Within the fictional moral parameters of a show that necessarily downplays the impact of violence, the conclusion reached is that middle-class corporate America is really in no position to be casting moral aspersions.

It is here, however, in a pivotal moment of possible awakening, that writer David Chase delivers a note of bathos warranting the show's critical acclaim, and one that also encapsulates a great dissonance at the heart of the American (and by extension, Western) identity. Jeannie Cusamano, Bruce Cusamano's wife, acknowledges the civility of the Soprano's fundraiser, but raises to her guests something far less forgivable than guns.

'. . . the bar,' she says, 'with that goombah Murano glass?'

The urgency with which the guests laugh suggests not so much amusement, but a sense of relief at being assured about the superiority of their tastes. Murano glass being a distinctive, colourful style of glassware encompassing various styles, including the marbled Calcedonio and the opaque, milk-coloured and hence-titled Lattimo glass, all of which were traditionally produced on the island of Murano that stands north-west of Venice, was maligned for many decades (it has more recently enjoyed a popular revival, with authentic glasses able to command several hundreds of pounds on resale sites).

'Goombah' being Italian-American slang for mob associates, the derision in Jeannie Cusamano's comment is self-evident, and carries with it a puritanism, both literal (in the hangover of white, Presbyterian prejudice towards Catholic culture) and more metaphorical (in the general insipidness that is conflated with respectability in the minds of America's established middle class towards the gauche, exuberant tastes of their immigrant neighbours). According to the rules of the dominant group, it is not possible for alternative tastes to exist alongside one another in a horizontal fashion, but for these tastes to be ranked according to their place in a social hierarchy.

Carmela and Tony's choice of glassware being mentioned in a wider conversation about the family's criminal connections illustrates how 'poor taste' is not just considered evidence of stupidity and ignorance, but also a *moral* shortcoming: Murano glass (at that time at least) almost constituting a crime worse than murder. This egregious episode is not lost on Melfi, who insists that she likes Murano glass, a view I hold myself: though specifically, the Millefiori or 'thousand flower' glass that my nan would always bring back from her holidays in the form of paperweights, vases and cups, inlaid with delicate nuggets of brightly coloured paint.

In this sense, the mob premise of *The Sopranos* affords David Chase the opportunity to pose questions about cultural capital and taste, through characters who are cash rich and full of notoriety, but whose cultural standing places them far outside the realm of respectable American society. This is not to suggest that the social estrangement that the characters experience constitutes something equal to impoverishment, but simply to highlight how much more challenging it is to escape impoverishment under those circumstances, and the falsity that underscores the idea of the American Dream. The show's success hinges on the relatability of this experience and the sense of alienation felt by so many excluded from the formal avenues of power and success. Gang violence might be a more extreme prism through which to explore this phenomenon, but the central truth, which forms the basis of Tony's fundamental tragic flaw, is one that millions of people can comfortably relate to.

Chapter Three

Fashion

Look in the mirror and take one thing off

COCO CHANEL

The voyeuristic gaze that had got me through hundreds of hours working as a tutor and a nanny would continue into my next job in magazine publishing, where I would show up each day wearing outfits cobbled together from what I owned, and trying to ignore the titters from colleagues whose own small pride in having accumulated the latest fashions always seemed pitiful to me anyway. I got the job through a contact after years of doing unpaid writing pieces for other magazines, suggesting that the official recruitment processes found online would never garner a real job, at least in that particular field, and that it was only by meeting people that I stood a chance of being counted – slowly and painfully exposing myself to the right crowds over a long period of time, and in a manner that I found uncomfortable and challenging, being as I am socially awkward and not that good in large groups. On my first day I wore a beige shirt and an orange, pleated, leopard-print knee-length skirt, in each case, items given to me by friends who did not want them, in what felt like the nearest approximation I had to something stylish. I was then living in a squat in Shadwell, East London, with people I did not know, and the process of getting ready involved having to hoist into my room a large broken mirror that had been left outside on an open passageway that ran along the roof of the building and into the property next door. This is also how you accessed the shower, meaning that I was forced to walk outside in my towel through the whole of winter. Somewhere still are the mirror photos of me bent down and trying to get a full scan of the weird outfit under the limited amount of light that came through the broken blinds and in the dim and mottled view of the corroded glass.

My starting salary, even in London, was £15,000. For that sum, I would process the paperwork connected to the large salary of my boss, as well as his expenses, which included receipts for clothes, hotel suites in Paris, Milan and New York, and huge rounds of drinks for contacts across the industry. In his spare time this man worked as a guerrilla poet, hijacking public advertising spaces (that he paid for) with aphoristic clauses about sadness, death, poverty and alienation. He wore blue-collar work jackets, brushed cotton slacks, loose-fitting black T-shirts and brothel creeper shoes, in a look that said 'middle-aged Rimbaud aspirant'. While riding around in taxis he would have me order for him most days, he would be scrawling poetry in his Moleskine, making plans for new art installations in Sharpie pen and spurning laptops and iPads.

He was often thumbing through thrifted copies of French books and doing poetry recitals via Skype. His heroes were Robert Burns, e. e. cummings and Tilda Swinton. Sometimes he would nudge me and try to goad me into mocking one of our colleagues, who often showed up to work wearing high heels and carrying a handbag – something he judged to be tasteless and embarrassing. For a while he wanted us to start a poetry pamphlet together.

Over the following few years I encountered many, albeit less extreme examples of a type similar to my boss, in that they were wealthy and upwardly mobile but apparently keen to conceal their lucrative place in an exploitative economy through aesthetic choices of a more austere impression. It was a wholesale phenomenon. Excepting a few fascinating flourishes, the 2010s was a decade defined by styles of an incredibly dour and unremarkable character, centred around a fashion masquerading as anything but; a style that spurned style, and an approach to clothing that seemed to shy away from people's gaze, while also being wholly dependent on it for oxygen.

This oh-so-alluring dance between yearned-for attention and its opposite would be referred to as *normcore* – the sartorial equivalent to the ubiquitous grey paint trend mentioned previously, or at least its contemporary, with a similar emphasis on the subdued, the understated and of course, the tasteful. A portmanteau combining 'normal' and 'hardcore', the term was first coined by the cartoonist Ryan Estrada in the webcomic *Templar, AZ* in 2008.[1] Very quickly it would be adopted around the world to describe that which rejected self-expression, and along with it, any and all forms of ostentation, including: loud colours, tight fits and obvious brand logos. Instead, more overt expressions of personal style were replaced by canvas plimsolls, plain white T-shirts, embellishment-free pullovers and straight-cut jeans.

As a trend, normcore was far more ubiquitous than minimalist fads that had gone before it. If the Beatniks of the mid-twentieth century had insisted on a simple, monochromatic style of dress, then it was also confined to a fringe movement of fashionable intellectuals and artists. Normcore, by contrast, would become, well, the norm, working its way into almost every corner of society and ultimately transforming conventional ideas of what constituted even formal attire and office wear, to the point that most corporate workplaces today permit their staff to wear jeans and T-shirts, or at least some variation on 'business casual'. In many ways, then, I could not have chosen a more boring time to take that job and it was only because nowhere else would have me that I spent almost three years in those offices.

Breton bores

During that time I would lope back to the squat of an evening carrying a rucksack that usually contained dinner ingredients of cottage cheese and roasting potatoes. The route led me past a store situated close to the old mice-riddled flat in Shoreditch (the landlord by that point had priced us out), whose stock-in-trade was functional homewares and fashions. From unwrapped Marseilles soaps, to horsehair brushes and dyed blue cotton overalls, the store's vast tiled rooms were always filled with shoppers pouring in from nearby advertising offices, keen to stock up on items for a more bucolic existence that they were cultivating in the nearby villages of Walthamstow and East Ham. Having understood that such items now constituted a form of luxury, I saved my meagre earnings from the magazine one Christmas to buy gifts of a similar style for my family. The look of bemused horror on their faces will forever be etched on my memory, as they peeled back the paper, revealing items of an imposed austerity that the past half-a-century had been spent trying to escape: non-mechanical cooking implements, herbal toothpastes, shapeless garments whose dyes required handwashing, cotton handkerchiefs, bird whistles, cotton string bags, tool belts, pinafores, tin cups, bottle brushes, yarn.

As one friend put it, normcore, which was first observed in the late 2000s, and extends its reach far into the present day, is possibly the longest-standing fashion trend ever to occur. But the more I reflect on this observation, the more it seems to me that considering normcore a trend in and of itself would be an error. All factors considered, it is far more apt to describe normcore as the point at which fashion, in as far as it encompassed personal or social identity – of using clothing to assert an idea of the self or to pledge allegiance to a given subculture, group or movement – ceased to exist altogether. In this sense, normcore marked the point at which fashion finally conceded to its other, far more depressing definition, as a billion-dollar industry predicated on conformity and status anxiety alone.

Normcore might have been everywhere, but very few would become masters of its art. And in fact, if it was not a trend then it became clear that normcore really constituted more of a proficiency than anything else. Because of the death knell that it spelled for so much variety and cultural expression, the idea was not so much a given style or look, as the tacit communication of an acquired wisdom through the very specific choice of brand, cut and material you were wearing.

From an initial preference for straight-cut jeans and outdoor jackets, to a mass, cultural obsession with cotton thread counts and dye processes, but also specific cuts of trouser, hemlines, weaves of denim, and types of wool, what mattered wasn't so much the choice of item, just whether or not it was produced under the very particular set of conditions approved by those in the know. These conditions might include processes that prioritised sustainability, for example, but the environmental impact was a secondary concern to the level of initiation being conveyed.

By contrast, almost any other trend of the past, from the countercultural to the distinctly bourgeois, was about expression. A goth, for example, could achieve their ends through the application of black eyeliner and black clothes dye; but equally, too, and from a wholly different perspective, even the yuppie or the preppy could achieve their ends through a pair of charity-shop brogues and an argyle sweater. These trends were first and foremost costumes, and while certain social and economic factors might have contributed to their creation, once birthed, they enjoyed a life untethered from their origins, and somewhat also untethered from any wider economic conditions, becoming identities that a person was free to assume and adopt based on cultural affinity or preference. Normcore was nothing but proximity to the deciders of good taste – a trend that actively spurned costume, and replaced it with a fixation on the tacit signifiers of erudition whose focal point became ever-more minute. Normcore carried no tangential associations with music, art, film or other modes of cultural expression, and as such, had no relation to the corporate-spurning slouchy styles of indie or grunge; nor the slick, peacocking styles of latter-day streetwear.

In this sense, trends prior to normcore were a way of putting one's stake in the ground, of declaring to the world a certain set of ideological beliefs and assumptions. Normcore, by contrast, was considered to be above subjective judgements, its preferences posited instead as universally good and unassailable: a fashion of undisputed quality triumphing over fleeting fads. It might therefore be considered the outward expression of a liberal tendency more broadly, and a centre-left politics that had come to assume the commonsensical position, rather than being considered one of multiple competing, but legitimate, forms of political belief. If the pluralism of democracy had partially faltered and given way to a dogmatic centre that considered itself to be beyond reproach and representative of all that was correct and sensible, then fashion – once consisting of so many opposing styles and subcultures – would appear to have succumbed to a similar logic, not of 'right' versus 'left', but of 'right' versus 'wrong'. As a result, even the very idea of luxury was transformed, as the distinct and expressive styles of fashion houses such as Chanel, Dior, Prada and Versace, came to be usurped as the first and last word in splendour by brands offering well-tailored everyday items that conformed to the highly functional modes of taste traditionally championed by the white middle classes of Northern (rather than Southern, predominantly Catholic) Europe – brands such as Margaret

Howell, A.P.C. and Studio Nicholson. Actor siblings the Olsen Twins would launch The Row, doubtless inspired by a certain strain of imperialist French chic encountered during Mary-Kate Olsen's marriage to Nicolas Sarkozy's brother, and beloved of the fashion crowd due its trading in various items of beige, grey and black. While Phoebe Philo, the fashion designer and former creative director of Celine, would be granted doyen status and give rise to a whole new form of fashion follower, one that the industry publication *Business of Fashion* misguidedly termed the 'Philophile' and identified by its love of oversized men's shirts, tailored trousers and turtleneck sweaters.[2] Meanwhile, normcore's more affordable purveyors – mass-market stores such as COS, Arket and Everlane – would steadily supplant the fad fashion retailers of the past to become the *de facto* outfitters of the professional middle-class across America and much of Western Europe.

The shift would be narrated with a certain sanctimony, as the obvious entrapments of wealth and decadence were replaced by items of *quality*. When described on the pages of the fashion magazines, in the video hauls that littered YouTube and in the TV segments urging viewers to *invest* in a *few key pieces* – mean-spirited fashion editors, paid to humiliate the clueless masses and cooing over one black cotton smock after another – would use one word more than any other: *plain*. A plain white T-shirt, a simple pair of jeans, a modest camel-coloured raincoat, a classic pair of trainers, and an understated cashmere scarf. This is what we were charged with buying as we became reframed as dumb pupils of a fashion discipline, reduced to its most basic terms.

What always struck me too about that word 'plain' was

the great deal of complexity that it belied. Often the plainest white T-shirt was one that contained a world of subtle indicators – not the multipack item bought from the supermarket, but the very particular boxy cut, with crew-neckline, brushed cotton, loose sleeves. Plain did not mean that which was easy and accessible, but that which carried a degree of design prestige. Like the functional, mid-century design objects that had been commoditised beyond recognition by interiors and lifestyle magazines, these 'plain' pieces had also become today's big ticket items.

None of which is to say that I prefer, nor make any apologies for, the rootless, swirling, multiplying madness of a free-market production cycle and its reliance on dehumanising labour conditions. I find the plastic landfill culture of the late twentieth century and early twenty-first century horrifying in its threat to global ecosystems. But the simplicity lauded by these new industries of taste – industries that were making enormous profits out of exploiting people's consumer anxieties, and in the process, creating a new class of yuppie that would exemplify the lifestyle peddled to everybody else – without any change in the economic conditions that would allow for the true spirit of minimalism and frugality to be revived at scale and adopted by everyone, amounted to little more than a farce. In the virtual terrain of consumer capitalism, with its own internal laws of morality, the slack-wearing market shopper with a push-bike would enjoy a certain purity of conscience above the person forced by economic necessity into wearing synthetic clothing from affordable high-street retailers.

High street horror

The sci-fi film *Under the Skin* (dir., Jonathan Glazer, 2013), always struck me for its peculiar comment on the nature of identity, fashion and the dynamics of taste. The film adapts a novel of the same name, and one that I love. Written by British author Michel Faber and published in 2002, *Under the Skin* the text, tells the story of an extraterrestrial named Isserley (anonymous in the film adaptation), whose travails have been widely read as an allegory for sex work, and whose dislocation, an allegory for immigration. Driving day after day along the vast, desolate roads leading to Inverness, Isserley is tasked with picking up and hunting hitchhikers, drugging them and returning them to a remote compound, where they are fattened up and farmed off for meat. This dimension of the story is much more explicit in the book, while its portrayal in the film is more abstract and mysterious. Throughout the film, Scarlett Johansson's Isserley character – a meek, quiet, almost mute figure – wears a vacant stare that is unsettling, while the men that she encounters range from the innocent and unassuming to the more predatory. For much of the film, director Glazer shoots Johansson in public settings and from a distance, so that the reactions we observe are natural, from passers-by who seem to have no prior awareness of their involvement in the film, or the presence of a Hollywood movie star. It is a testament to the people of Glasgow that within seconds of Johansson falling to the ground, in a scene that has been endlessly memefied and shared online, an elderly man, two teenage boys and several women in rain jackets surround her, offering a hand in help.

In this scene and in others, Johansson is dressed in clothes that are commonly sold in the cheaper high-street retail chains, market stalls or charity shops of modern Britain. She wears a cerise-pink top, a barely concealed synthetic lace bra, a faux fur jacket – fixed at the waist with a hook-and-eye fastening – tight elastic jeans or 'jeggings', in a faded, mottled blue print, and a pair of fur-lined, conical-heeled boots. Crucially, the image created by this look is not one of abject or exaggerated hardship – this is not Charlize Theron performing the role of Aileen Wuornos in *Monster* (2003), and there are no prosthetics, wigs or prize-winning makeup jobs to speak of. Yet the impact is arguably more profound and uncanny on account of its slightness, and as a result of only making the smallest of adjustments to the usual socioeconomic programming. So degrading and dispiriting are the methods of modern advertising, the demand for cultural capital and the propaganda methods of the contemporary fashion industry, that the true opposite of a Hollywood movie star is not the Victorian vagabond or the street urchin of before, but *us*: the synthetic fibre-wearing masses. There seems to be nothing more improbable than Scarlett Johansson being a woman of average income forced to shop on the British high street, as we contend with the urge to take a hold of the dislocated movie star who has wondered far off course and guide her back to safety. We are being invited to consider our own gaze and how far it might have been infected by prejudices of class and social status.

With every interaction between Johansson's character and the people she meets, the line between prey and victim is blurred, and it is not always clear where our sympathies should lie. This dimension is stressed in the Glazer version, with

Johansson picking up one client whose disabilities are visible. In the book, Isserley has the power to seduce these men, but she is also vulnerable to their predations, as each eyes up the other, measuring their chances, assessing their ability to meet their own ends. Here we are also supplied the men's internal monologues, which range from the sweet and sympathetic, to the baldly sexual and desirous. With only the exception of one male victim, all are prone to scouring Isserley's body, admiring the size of her breasts, processing the oddities in her movement, and looking for clues for an invitation to sex. Throughout, and due to the accounts of how these men are optimised for consumption once they have been harvested, themes of exploitation and desensitisation are woven into a narrative that comments on several issues relevant to modern developed societies, among them industrial-scale farming, casual labour and the immiseration of working people. But what strikes me in the adaptation from text to film, and particularly in the casting of Johansson, is Glazer's ambition to tease out the tension between personhood and presentation. If the title *Under the Skin* urges us to question the vast subjectivity of emotion, experience and expectation that is often overlooked when we sexualise and objectify the other, then in the translation to film, this question also extends to the judgements that are made of people's clothing, and the class signifiers contained therein, with even the most recognisable of people unable to outshine the symbolic weight of what they wear.

Clothing can indicate vulnerability and/or power, and the implications of this go beyond mere feeling. In *Under the Skin*, the Johansson character indicates how certain styles of clothing are often read as the person being permissible for exploitation, and not only on account of their apparent affordability or how 'revealing' and 'suggestive' they might be. Arguably, the main source of the character's vulnerability resides in the oddness of her look. Despite being comprised of elements that I have only just now praised for their ubiquity and faithfulness to modern life, the particular arrangement of the outfit, and its collision with a hairstyle that is just slightly *off* – a little too voluminous and shaggy perhaps for someone of her age and situation – indicates a degree of social estrangement. Whether it registers consciously with us or not, part of the character's eeriness resides in the demonstrative lack of cultural understanding, or taste. And it is this, more so than the implication of poverty (though the two are obviously interlinked and often inextricable), that is also the cause of abuse and exploitation. It is not just literal signifiers of economic plight or prosperity that determine a person's legitimacy, but the degree to which they are able to express an understanding of, or at least a desire to emulate, the dominant modes and styles.

Compare this to the character of Johnny, played by David Thewlis in the seminal Mike Leigh film *Naked* (1993). Johnny's story is one of endless chances, and is almost picaresque in its telling of the speed and the casualness with which he flits from one opportunity to the next, always riding on the kindness of strangers. Through a sort of prodigious command of the English language, Johnny is able to bamboozle almost everybody he meets, in one of the most accurate and at times distressing accounts of misogyny and narcissism ever told on screen. But this film also demonstrates the currency of cultural capital; as Johnny's somewhat easy passage through life, following his attack on a woman in the street, is facilitated by his being a man, of course, but also his ability to reference literature, allude to intellectual subject matter and conform to a sort of neutral, inoffensive uniform of all-black. That Johnny is too reckless to harness this for anything other than the further exploitation of desperate people around him, is a comment on character rather than circumstance. Unlike Isserley, or her nameless film version, and unlike anyone prevented from developing certain modes of speech and demonstrations of confidence, Johnny, at the very least, has options.

Isserley's only recourse in a society that devalues women, and working-class women of a possible immigrant status in particular, is through her sexuality, or her *skin*, which might be enhanced through that second skin of what she chooses to wear. Without divulging too much of the film's ending, its example demonstrates the extreme consequences of failing to pass for the kind of person that our image obsessed society deems worthy of respect. This is something most working-class women will have understood tacitly since adolescence, as they learned to navigate a world of threats that often far outnumbered opportunities. We find ourselves returning to the example of Roz and Daphne in *Frasier*, and how money facilitates a certain degree of loud, sexual expression, necessarily downplayed or repressed by those who are far more liable to be exploited – Roz, Frasier's show producer and the affluent daughter of a politician who serves as the Attorney General, is sexually liberated and expressive in her style of dress, while Daphne, a domestic labourer, is much more unassuming and girly. Harnessing sexuality may be the only possible route to financial security for millions of women, and yet it must always be weighed against the possibility of violence. While knowing consciously that no woman's sexual exploitation is ever as a result of what she wears, most of us will have nevertheless internalised the dread and shame of that potential experience in ways that determine our choice of clothing. Queer people learn to do the same, as do people of colour adept at decoding situations, and responding in kind; knowing as they do, that their choice of clothing can and often will be retroactively used as justification for discrimination, arrest, or worse.

The hoodie as fall guy

The shooting of Trayvon Martin in 2012 is one of the most significant events in America's history of racial oppression and also foregrounds a tendency to deflect accusations of bigotry and racism with talk of clothing, and taste. Martin was a teenager and schoolboy killed at the hands of a twenty-nine-year-old man called George Zimmerman, in what the latter claimed to be an act of self-defence. Zimmerman's testimony included mention of a hoodie that Martin was wearing, as he walked back to his stepmother's property in the gated community of The Retreat at Twin Lakes in Sanford, Florida, after purchasing a packet of Skittles and a watermelon soda from a nearby store. In the course of the trial and beyond, Martin's hoodie became an emblem of the prejudice and double standards that black people face daily, in America and beyond.

Though Zimmerman later implied that dark hoodies had been flagged as an indication of wrongdoing by the local Neighbourhood Watch programme, its initial mention was in response to a police question about what Martin was wearing, in a call made by Zimmerman to the local force in the moments before the trigger was pulled. Nevertheless, and as a cross-examiner later stressed, Martin was also wearing light trousers, distinguishing his from the all-black outfits that the Neighbourhood Watch programme's absurd trial-by-clothing policy had nevertheless identified as threatening (I am reluctant to even mention this detail, given that there can be no concession made to people being profiled for their everyday choices of dress.) The other important detail is that it was raining and that almost anyone spotted in the region of Sanford at that time would have been seen wearing some form of protection from the elements. That Zimmerman would proceed to embark on a career painting Confederate flags is suggestive of the man's politics. This only stresses the urgency of the question: why had discussion of a hoodie – worn in the rain, by a teenager returning from buying himself a snack – ever been allowed, and what did it tell us about the ways in which the language of prejudice and discrimination had evolved?

Mention of the hoodie curried favour with the right-wing press. Staggeringly, soon after Martin was killed, Fox News anchor Geraldo Rivera claimed that Martin's death had been in part caused by his 'gangster-style clothing', before adding: 'I am urging the parents of black and Latino youngsters particularly to not let their children go out wearing hoodies.' While it was beyond the pale for Zimmerman's sympathisers to admit the truth about how they felt – that Martin's skin colour was cause enough for suspicion – it was apparently OK to question his style of clothing. Similar bigotries, of course, and as mentioned above, occur in the discussion of violence against women, and the question of how items of clothing may be the cause of unwanted attentions from men. But if we dispel whatever associations we might have been taught to have of these items – short skirts, low-cut tops, hoodies, caps – and see them only as expressions of a personal preference and cultural expression, their inclusion in discussions about the causes of violent crime may be read as a way of approving violence against particular individuals and groups.

This was not the first time the hoodie had featured in political discourse, and certainly not the first time an item of clothing had been presumed by those in power to be the cause of society's ills. A few years earlier, British politics had witnessed its own hoodie-related event when the leader of the Conservative Party (and later British prime minister) David Cameron addressed an audience at a conference held by his party's 'social justice task force' in 2006. In what would be dubbed the 'hug a hoodie speech', due to Cameron proposing a radical new crime-tackling approach based on instilling 'good, honest' values in the homes of deprived kids, he said: ' . . . we, the people in suits, often see the hoodies as aggressive', before elaborating on his plan to bring social cohesion to the streets of Britain. Cameron never actually used the phrase 'hug a hoodie', which was actually an invention of a Labour Party press release written in the days afterwards, though the name came to be synonymous with his tenure in government.

Reading it back, the divisional rhetoric is barely concealed, with Cameron creating a shared identity both among suit wearers and their supposed opposite. What had been framed as an attempt to banish old divisions of race and class, only reinstated those divisions under the guise of style, or taste. Overt discrimination in the form of class prejudice and racism had been transferred to the language of sartorial codes. Cameron did this by boldly conflating people with their clothing, insinuating a lack of separation between the item and the wearer, such that we might encounter, or be encountered, as a *suit with a soul* or a *hoodie with a heart*. The upper middle class had been rebranded a suit, the worker, a hoodie. A new form of 'us and them' had emerged, only it evaded accusations of outright bigotry by claiming to be a far more fair and pragmatic assessment of respectability, hard work and sound presentation. This was a society that would dole out rewards based on merit, remunerating those among us prepared to convey ourselves with dignity and good sense – that is, *the tasteful* – and rightly punishing those who weren't. We had once again found ourselves in that maddening swirl of rhetoric, of class as taste and taste as class, with both being considered an extension of a person's character and their willingness to contribute to the capitalist society.

Perhaps more relevant to the case of Trayvon Martin however, and certainly America's own complex and perverse relationship with the hoodie, came ten years before Cameron's speech, during the 1996 US presidential election campaigns fought between our friend Bill Clinton and his opponent, Bob Dole. During that campaign, the Democratic candidate, in a weekly radio segment aimed at updating the American public on his various election pledges, delivered a litany of appeals to the country's anxious middle class, and specifically, its middle-class parents. Before its adoption as shorthand for a strain of uppity proto-Karen in twinsets and pearls, the 'Soccer Mom' had been identified as a target Democrat voter. Whether or not such a demographic existed in reality, or was an invention of pollsters and strategists, remains unclear, but what we know at least was that it was ostensibly white, more secular in its beliefs than one might assume of a Republican housewife, and heavily invested in its child's success. For this group of people, whether real or imagined, Clinton vowed to impose school uniforms, for the purposes of delivering greater emphasis on discipline and education, and with the added boon of achieving greater equanimity between young people who were being thrown together in classrooms all across America.

What was strange about Clinton's election pledge was the justification that he provided, saying in that same radio broadcast, that ' . . . if it means that teenagers will stop killing each other over designer jackets . . . then our public schools should be able to require their students to wear school uniforms'.

Clinton provided no further detail or clarification of what he meant, and the vagueness speaks to just how pervasive the belief must have been, that fashion trends really were the cause of serious crime. Clinton was in fact referring to the killing of seventeen-year-old Charles 'Chuckie' Marsh Jr. In December 1995, Marsh Jr., who was a black teenager, had been stood among friends near his school, when they had been approached by two gunmen in balaclavas wanting to steal a nearby teen's Eddie Bauer jacket. Eddie Bauer was an outdoor apparel brand carrying a Northwest Pacific, mountaineer prestige, whose jackets had become an object of consumer desire among younger people during the mid-1990s, partly because of how they had been ironically adopted by musicians and celebrities. For example, the rappers Mase and Jadakiss released the track '24 Hours to Live', which included a name-check of the SUV that the company created in collaboration with Ford: 'Load the three power, hop in the Eddie Bauer'. According to reports, Marsh Jr. was the unintended victim of the shooter, and was not wearing the jacket in question.

Marsh Jr. was killed in the altercation and the perpetrator was never caught, meaning that their exact motives are still unknown. Clinton seized on the anger and frustration caused by that event in a bid to secure a second term in office. What we do know about school shootings, however, is that they are a result of law-making that facilitates easy access to firearms, and any violence in schools is usually the product of a deep-seated tension created by economic inequality and the social resentments that they create. Clinton's statement and the one made later by David Cameron in the UK, not to mention countless others made casually by the media in the years since, offloaded onto a jacket, or a hoodie, or a pair of trainers, the weight of responsibility for a boy's death and countless other crimes as well.

This comment and election pledge indicated a common tendency to confuse the object for the far bigger, systemic issues that it represents, such as inequality, racial tension, rampant and unchecked consumer desire and status anxiety. It also indicated a liberal tendency to blame policy failures on their fallouts. School uniforms are a practical way of maintaining the delusion of equality for the few short hours that exist between first bell and last, but until the causes of that latent disorder are addressed, new symbols of desire and projection will always emerge. The flipside of this is that people unwilling to forfeit the luxuries they enjoy and which depend on the subjugation of others, but who like to soothe themselves with the belief that they are fighting for a better world – what I am tempted to refer to as the liberal condition, or malady, in general – often believe that they can achieve the latter through symbolism alone. There can be jeopardy in a symbol, as was revealed in a scandal in which it was found that a T-shirt brandishing the slogan 'this is what a feminist looks like', issued by the feminist campaign group The Fawcett Society, had been manufactured by cheap labour in Mauritius where workers (who were predominantly women), were paid as little as 62p an hour. The Fawcett Society insisted the shirts were made to ethical standards, but as many recognised at the time, these standards were not what would be considered acceptable by Western standards, and whilst no doubt was cast on the sincerity of the campaign, the media storm revealed the importance of looking beyond words.

What's more, allowing the symbol of clothing to carry the burden of stigma – which has not disappeared but just been denied and displaced – creates a climate in which personal dress more readily becomes a matter of life or death. Veer too far from the pervasive modes of taste dictated by those in power and one can expect to be the subject of suspicion, humiliation and in some cases, attack. In Hilton Als's essay collection *White Girls* (2013), the critic and journalist speaks about the self-effacement that black writers are often required to adopt; a principle that applies just as much to clothing as any other aspect of life. Using the figure of the pious mother figure in black literature to illustrate his point, Als writes that the mask of piety ' . . . is the one thing standing between her children and death. Yes sir, yes ma'am, she says from behind the mask. And, with eyes lowered, Please, sir, do not kill my children.' The symbol of the mask is useful, allowing us to see how clothing forms a literal façade of conformity and submission to those in power. *I am urging the parents of black and Latino youngsters particularly to not let their children go out wearing hoodies.*

In a secular society, or at least in situations when a cursory effort must be made to uphold a semblance of rationality despite a clear ideological agenda (as in the case of Fox News), the question of piety has shifted away from the world of action, and on to the world of appearances. Christian sanctimony had been used for centuries to justify the crimes of colonialism and censure other cultures. And while it might have ceased to be the primary, functioning belief system in most Western countries, its attitudes have nevertheless been absorbed into a language of decency and good taste. To see how prejudices of style have become absorbed and naturalised under a new form of secular morality, one need only watch shows aimed at trying to rehabilitate 'wayward' people through the transformation of their clothing, a phenomenon that reached fever pitch in the late 1990s and early 2000s with shows like *Ladette to Lady* (2005–10), *Style Her Famous* (2006–9), and *From G's to Gents* (2008–9).

The purpose of these shows was to educate the viewer, as much as the participant. In these, like the TV fashion segments mentioned previously, aimed at steering us towards making more tasteful choices in clothing, was an idea of fashion as a set of rules, divergence from which might also constitute a more profound transgression of respectable society. The truth is, and despite my misgivings about the fashion industry, I love clothes and would have liked to make them. I believe not only in the right of everyone to dress how they want and without concern for how other people might judge them, but also the essential role of clothing in allowing us to explore and establish our identities. So extensive is the effort to naturalise certain forms of bigotry and discrimination – to present them instead as rational responses to moral failings – that we are discouraged from ever interrogating their place in a society and its politics. It is perhaps why fashion is such a dirty word in certain circles, as any serious, intellectual attention paid to it inevitably throws up a million questions about authority, but also about race, sex, gender and identity. In answering the question of how a fascinating discipline uniting art, design, technology and cultural anthropology, had been reduced to a term of facile preoccupation, whose followers constituted 'victims', we actually arrive at several fascinating discoveries that unveil so much about the power structures that underscore modern life. Because knowingly or not, fashion is something we all participate in, even those of us wearing the three-pack plain polo-shirts bought for us by our wives, or the prudes who insist on wearing only 'plain' items of a timeless character. Paradoxically, the dads loping moodily around the aisles of Target and Marks and Spencer might just be the most anxious and image-conscious of all, their mode of style, unassuming on the face of it, having evolved over many decades to placate the terrified concern of attracting any unwanted interrogation of their gender or sexual orientation.

If homes are the private domain, reflective of our most deeply held ideas about comfort, familiarity and safety, then clothes represent the version of ourselves that we choose to present to the world. In Freud's model of the psyche, composed of ego, superego and id, it is the first of these that would seem to relate most to fashion: the part of ourselves that deals in reality, and must negotiate between the more libidinal urges of the animal psyche (or id), and the expectations that we inherit as members of a society (the superego). Contained behind the doors of each and every one of our wardrobes then, are clues as to how this society has shaped us, and how we have chosen to respond in turn; of what our hopes, dreams and fears might be, as well as the kinds of people that we might want to be associated with or attract.

Only many years after leaving the magazine and from studying certain specific cases, was I able to understand how power is subtly exerted through fashion, and often in ways that are designed to seem counterintuitive and nonsensical to those on the outside. For the top-down morality to work, for those in power to be able to skilfully conceal bigotries through a language of aesthetic concern, and for the rest of us to believe in this reasoning, the styles of the dominant class must remain somewhat elusive. In the way of religion and the promise of the afterlife, style and acceptance are never destinations one reaches, but always yearns for and seeks to attain through continual study, maintenance and up-keep. What's more, the dynamic of power becomes more compelling when it appears to be absolute and universal, as opposed to a tussle between small and fallible human beings. For this reason it must develop a sort of camouflage, making it detectable to those in the know, and almost invisible to everyone else; a stealthy force that exerts itself quietly and in ways that we can often feel, even if we cannot understand.

The narcissism of small differences

To maintain an atmosphere of competition and curiosity, and to deflect suspicion away from the idea of nepotism and favourable treatment, a complex system of distinction emerges. In this regard, normcore recalls a trend that occurred in the nineteenth century, when the capitalist class yearned to be taken as seriously as, or even to usurp the social dominance of the aristocracy. The status anxiety of the bourgeoisie would lead to a paradoxical tendency in which it ultimately rejected the more frivolous tastes that had reigned supreme during the earlier Regency era, such as the Baroque and Rococo, with its ornate embellishments and exaggerated silhouettes, choosing instead to favour styles of a more pared back and modest variety.

This was exemplified by one particular item, which Queen Victoria's eldest son himself, the future King Edward VII, adopted, and perhaps in response to the threat of that ascendent middle-class. Prince Edward, as he was called then, first encountered the tuxedo – a shorter, more boxy alternative to the tailcoat that had been popular among affluent men in Britain during the first half of the nineteenth-century – during a visit to America, land of the self-made and entrepreneurial. He commissioned a replica from his Savile Row tailors, Henry Poole & Co, in 1865, starting the biggest trend in men's fashion in Britain since breeches and tasselled hessian boots. Here, the tuxedo would be called the dinner jacket, and it would symbolise a sort of relaxed modernity and arcane knowledge possessed only by the metropolitan circles who rejected the pomposity of a bygone age. For the aspirant class, it would also signal a quiet assuredness that would be useful in helping to navigate the tricky but potentially very lucrative waters of nineteenth-century high society, showing as it did a certain ease and assuredness: a jacket that openly scorned all that was ostentatious and served as a sort of mask to conceal the status anxieties that were still rife.

The point of the dinner jacket, much like the slacks and worker jackets of today, was to signal a degree of initiation. Many popular histories attribute its evolution to the relaxation of formality as an inevitable consequence of modernity. But to protect one's own lot during a time of vast economic upheaval, wealthy individuals would also be required to adopt certain styles in an effort to blend in. No sooner had the upwardly mobile decoded the rules and aesthetic preferences of those in charge, than new rules would be required to exclude the next cohort of aspirants.

On the one hand then, those with established power have often had to conceal their position. The efforts of the nineteenth century aristocracy to conceal their wealth in this way, and particularly following the reverberations of the French Revolution, are similar in many ways to the wealthy heirs of today who work as fashion models or artists and pose in tracksuits, trainers and install gold teeth. At the same time, forms of distinction for the aspiring class are required to become ever more niche, ever more complex and ever more indiscernible to the naked eye in order to keep one's cards close to one's chest, in a game of complex social manoeuvring. To put it even more bluntly than that, a climate of rampant interpersonal competition necessitates a culture of increasingly petty proportions, and this only becomes more exaggerated in an age of so much visual information and constant sharing. This is what Freud referred to as 'the narcissism of small differences', put forward in *Civilisation and its Discontents* (1930), in that case being used to describe the petty disputes and tensions that are prone to arise between neighbouring communities of a similar character in order to achieve quiet social dominance. The term has since evolved to describe various phenomena in which people attribute great importance to tiny discrepancies of taste and consumer choice; a tendency that is perhaps nowhere more effectively captured than in the 'business card' scene in Mary Harron's 2000 film adaptation of the Bret Easton Ellis novel *American Psycho,* in which the protagonist Patrick Bateman and his fellow demonic bankers enter into an egoistic display of the paper weight, kerning and ink used on their networking accoutrements. With the digital 'creative' ad or tech person now a contender for Patrick Bateman status in a society where he is rich but required to also downplay it, a similar tendency might be observed in the jostling between those who shop at Toast and deliberate as to the very particular shade of ecru dungarees that they should purchase; or the readers of *Hypebeast* and *Highsnobiety,* anxiously reading up on the latest consensus on crepe versus rubber soles.

It is the domain of the so-called tech 'creative' where the phenomenon of *crew-neck capitalism* has also emerged, a term first coined by the sociologist David Beer.[3] This refers to a tendency mentioned previously, and connected with normcore, of corporations allowing for a more relaxed and casual style of dress. This tendency would be heralded by the tech industry, which underwent a vast expansion in the late 2000s, around the same time that the global banking sector faced arguably the biggest crisis in its history. While the latter was the birthplace of the eighties yuppie, and therefore represented a form of emancipation for go-getting careerists, the tech industry would birth a far more self-effacing capitalist, one who seemed actively to reject any indication of its wealth or power through dress. Perhaps this was on account of the tech industry being far more reliant on consumer participation than the banking sector, and therefore requiring a far more affable outward appearance. The super-monopolies that were being created in the shape of Google, Apple, Amazon and Facebook, all required a public image that was variously cool, or friendly, or zany, and this would be nowhere more visible than in the style of dress that their workers would be forced to adopt, creating its own slew of speculative op-eds and rumour mills as to the purported existence of 'shoeless offices'.[4] The Hugo Boss suit, much like the tailcoat 150 years before it, would be found dead at the hands of a terry-cloth sweater.

These companies had originated on the West Coast of America, where the hangover of a sixties counterculture met with capitalism, creating entities that would at least be seen to spurn the corporate codes of the past. Part of Steve Jobs's appeal lay in his presentation as an auteur, rather than the brash, money-hungry capitalist of the Reagan era with its Trumpian monsters. Jobs was a man who dressed more like the playwright Samuel Beckett or the philosopher Michel Foucault than Michael Douglas in *Wall Street* (1987): black turtlenecks, rimless glasses, straight-cut jeans. Like the midnight-blue wainscoting of Soho House, he represented the assurance that one could reconcile mercenary greed with the desire to be taken seriously as an artist and intellectual.

What followed was the creation of a new breed of capitalist in tracksuits, trainers, snapbacks and oversized T-shirts; a cartoonish rendering of the bedroom teenager, commanding a salary in some cases of several millions a year. Machine-learning graduates on starter salaries of £300,000 would arrive at work every day wearing the kind of looks that would be considered beyond the pale even for a teenager on their school's own-clothes day, and create the harmful illusion that workplaces were becoming more equal. Corporations started to brag about their 'horizontal structures', where hierarchies of power had ceased to exist, or at least insofar as allowing the bosses to wear something resembling their pyjamas every day, ride skateboards around the office and use the word 'bro'. Of course we know that nothing could be further from the truth, and that these corporations have been criticised for their exploitation of workers; from the work conditions of the Amazon warehouses and the enormous profits being made by its billionaire owner Jeff Bezos, to the vast army of 'blue collar', agency-based support staff employed in Google offices around the world to carry out the manual tasks of cleaning, cooking and security.

Against the norm

For all these reasons, normcore had initially baffled and then irked me, but its rise was, in many cases, paved with good intentions. It arrived at a time when the exploitative and unsustainable practices and mass-production methods of the fashion industry were rightly being exposed, and directed us towards fewer, more conscientious and functional purchases.

Its emergence coincided with a heightened public awareness of the harms caused by so-called 'fast fashion', among them, the mistreatment of workers, as well as the environmental cost of an industry that encourages the ready consumption and disposal of clothes and accessories. In this sense, it can be seen as the mainstream, mass adoption of rejected gimmickry, which represented the many excesses of late capitalism and its advertising machinery. Quality and taste came to be ever more aligned with that buzzword 'craftsmanship', which indicated slower production methods, organic and home-grown materials and the fair remuneration of tradespeople and artisans. But these noble intentions rarely factored in the realities of wage stagnation or the lack of disposable income experienced by most working people, not to mention the fact that the appearance of something more sustainable and ethical could equally be affected through the same methods of mechanical and mass production.

Clothes might be considered a reflection of a moral and ethical framework, in what presented itself as the perfect solution to the gnawing greed that contradicted the austere pledges of the artist and his lifestyle. We could have both, it seemed: the authenticity *and* the stuff, provided everything we wore was sustainable, made by artisans and cost £500. Normcore in this sense was also more of a void, or a negative reasoning, a trend that didn't so much exert itself or make specific demands, but in the shadow cast by it, made an emblem of societal rot out of a pink polyester bodycon dress. It sanctified certain, initiated consumers while vilifying others, allowing those with the appropriate means and knowledge to absolve themselves of their place in a consumer society that was always stirring up a sense of inadequacy and yearning.

This was one 'problem' with normcore, but the other related to the question of who was being posited as the norm by its insipid preferences. If we had once lived in a cycle of commerce dictated by intergenerational disputes over what might be considered desirable and appealing, then it was as if society had collectively arrived at one final and definitive answer: Jerry Seinfeld, a man who represented a sort of low-stakes utopia fixed at the end of the last century, when an air of optimism could still be felt by jobbing comedians who could nevertheless enjoy the spoils of a middle-class existence, including the ownership of several well-made sweater vests. On the one hand, the Internet, by making all of history available to us at the click of a button, was responsible for having sped up both the recurring cycles of nostalgia that had once been the driving machinery behind new fashion trends, and also the slow percolation of styles from the margins of society towards the mainstream, through word of mouth and the appropriation of subcultures by the fashion runway show. With each being presented via the flat, democratising surface of the screen, where hierarchies of cool and edginess had been razed, it was as if a choice paralysis had set in so far that we could only default to a style of dress that appeared to us at least as being the most plain, simple and 'universal' – judgements that are of course highly subjective and born of countless cultural prejudices.

For those required to conform to certain expectations set by the powerful in order to be accepted, and to survive, fashion is not an arena of joyfulness and play, but stress, insecurity and anguish. As a result, and against a backdrop of intense hypocrisy – of subjective judgements being posited as universal, and affordable consumer choices being subtly castigated by the fetishisation of their opposite – more overt expressions of wealth seem almost innocent. It is easy to see how a style of dress that is more explicit than the quiet, unassuming expressions of wealth that had been exemplified here, would emerge the more sympathetic and relatable; how, contrary to the famous adage supposedly spoken by Coco Chanel, that before leaving the house everyone should 'look in the mirror and take one thing off', we might instead start to feel like we wanted to put one or several more things on.

Two people come to mind when discussing this tendency, and both of them inordinately wealthy yet also widely adored by working people. They are linked, uncannily, by a particular style of dress, ostentatious in the extreme and yet symbolic of a certain, complex rebellion whose underpinnings are the final subject of this chapter.

Princess Diana and Rihanna might be very different in terms of their background and life experiences, but the role they occupy in the public imagination is in many ways comparable. Both represent a sort of defiance towards social expectation, and particularly expectations held towards women with fame. They both share a lineage with the film star Elizabeth Taylor, whose attitude of indifference came to be strangely epitomised in a ludicrous collection of jewellery – problematic of course for its inclusion of many diamonds, but which on the face of it formed part of an image that seemed frequently to mock the male gaze and stand firm in its brash and decidedly camp resistance.

Attracting more discussion, debate and media coverage than even Taylor's jewellery collection, however, was the dress designed by David and Elizabeth Emanuel for Princess Diana's wedding to Prince Charles in 1981. From its voluminous puffed sleeves, to its reputed use of ten thousand pearls and its twenty-five-foot train, the cumulus dress, which swamped the frail princess's size-ten frame, set a precedent throughout the 1980s and early 1990s for more romantic fashions, and wedding fashions in particular, marking a point of departure and antagonism with the era's other fixation on modernity, technological advancement and simplicity.

In choosing a style favoured by the eighteenth-century aristocracy, Diana was riding on the coat-tails of the New Romantic movement and also aligning herself with an imperialist cohort known for its exploitation of working people in Britain and abroad. For this reason, the following point must be heavily couched as only applying to the very strict and highly autocratic rules of taste dictated by the monarchy and its media machinery, rather than claiming Diana to be a champion of the people or absolving herself of involvement in one of the last and most decrepit imperialist projects.

The dress is said to have been directly inspired by the kitsch portraits of Queen Victoria by German artist Franz Xaver Winterhalter, characterised by an overabundance of saccharine frills, bows and hair tumbling over sloped shoulders. But within the framework of a royal wedding – a ritual spanning centuries and documented extensively to function as propaganda for the head of state – the dress did represent, in its own albeit unique and complicated way, a form of subversion. This only became more exaggerated with the passage of time and the emergence of Diana as a dissident voice within the monarchy and British establishment; a fact that made her earlier choice of wedding dress seem all the more defiant. Because, as described previously in the case of Edward VII, the Royal Family had, for many reasons and for many centuries by that point, been invested in protecting its status through a certain concealment of riches and its rebranding as servants of the people. This only became more urgent following the death of the Romanovs in 1918, but also with the existential crisis posed by decolonisation, in which it could no longer proudly declare itself the figurehead of empire. At the very least, the twentieth-century British monarchy was not lauding its wealth over the populace in quite the same way as King Louis XVI of France. Instead, the emphasis had been on public duty, with the Queen emerging a figure of assiduity. This in itself constituted an hypocrisy that Diana's more girlish choice of wedding dress only highlighted; the photos from her wedding day serving to humiliate the institution she was marrying into, reminding us in the most vivid terms possible of its hoarded excesses and colonial spoils. If Queen Victoria's son had begun the trend of normcore among the landed gentry, then that would come to an abrupt end in the thousand folds of silk that glided the length of St Paul's Cathedral on the morning of 29 July 1981.

Of course, none of this needed to be intentional nor obvious at the time, nor of course did it have to be by Diana's own design, which I strongly suspect it was not: the nineteen-year-old bride seemed to be in every way relishing her performance in the apparent climax of a Barbara Cartland-esque romance. The biopic *Spencer* (dir., Pablo Larrain, 2021) contains a scene in which the princess can be found trying on a succession of couture dresses, performing for the camera in the way of a fashion shoot. Far from finding this scene facile as many critics did, it communicated to me the central importance of clothes to the woman's celebrity. Fashion, and Diana's particular approach to it, formed a large part of a legend that was seldom allowed to speak, and indeed, as a result, the clothes often spoke for her.

Thirty-four years later, an heir to that earlier wedding dress would be born on the red carpet of the 2015 Met Gala in New York, when Rihanna emerged in an oversized yellow gown by the Chinese designer Guo Pei. The gown's train swamped Rihanna and almost the entirety of the carpet in its blanket of gold brocade. It was an aristocratic gesture by a black woman outside of a museum packed to the hilt with looted items from former American and European colonies, at an event hosted by a fashion industry whose entire purpose had until recently been to uphold standards of respectability enshrined by a white imperialism. For her performance at the Superbowl in 2022, Rihanna wore a floor-length red puffa coat after a style worn by the celebrated fashion editor Andre Leon Talley, an item of clothing that had come to represent an overthrowing of that pious mask referred to by Hilton Als, and the self-effacing costume that the black person in America had been forced to wear for centuries in the name of survival.

Chapter Four

Beauty

Less is More

UNKNOWN

It would be remiss of me to challenge the idea of good taste and not also stray from literary convention from time to time to discuss matters such as my own ass, for example, which is resplendent: properly big and beautiful and fat. After growing up in an age where under-nourished bodies were the cause of every magazine and TV show aimed at teenage girls, I feel duty-bound to say this, and to preserve in writing the fact of my wide, round, heavy cheeks that are textured like ana-glypta wallpaper (which is another love of mine and which I would also devote several pages to, would it not lead to you closing the book and never opening it again). My ass is also illusory, at one time seeming round and full, at others, angu-lar and powerful, depending on my stance. Such incoherence seems to be a point of fixation to the people who encounter it; the lucky few, as I like to think of them, one of whom, a man from California who took great pride in telling me about his education at the hands of celebrated gender studies writer and philosopher Judith Butler, felt the need to mention it the first time I was naked in front of him, complimenting it profusely and with an enthusiasm that I suspect he had learned to repress more publicly. This was not something he would share with the boys. But it was a compliment that was also laced with incredulity, as if my ass – *the ass*, as we have been schooled to think of it through a media intent on reducing women's bodies to a litany of parts – seemed to be at odds with the person. When pushed, he explained that it seemed incongruous with his impression of me as a writer from London, after encountering my work years previously.

It was here that the matter of writing a chapter on beauty was decided. Though I should state for the record that I was not offended by this comment, which was only meant as a compliment, just confused that any particular body should be considered more fitting, or expected, of the writing profession. There is, of course, a traditional image of the woman writer, forged in the minds of people perhaps around the time of Virginia Woolf and the Bloomsbury Group in Britain, of someone austere, wan and fragile. I was aware of this stereotype, of course – distantly, not too keenly – but perhaps I was naive about the extent to which students of celebrated philosophers would still subscribe to it.

The comment about my ass raised a point about the association that is drawn between physical attributes and economic groups, or professions. Not to mention how beauty and sexuality are often defined in opposition. When the class system relies on the impression that hierarchies of power and wealth are inevitable and meritocratic, every aspect of our material lives is judged according to how far it conforms to the aesthetic preferences of those in power. The physical body is no exception, and in fact, owing to the mechanisms of the advertising industry, carries the burden of respectability above even our physical dwellings, wardrobes or lifestyle choices – a very particular type of body becoming a status symbol and item in the wider 'asset' portfolio (no pun intended – in fact, that common phrase can tell us quite a lot), that we are forced to acquire in the name of selling ourselves in the job market. As a result, and owing to the logic of the corporate-professional sphere, the very real and present horror emerges of there being 'tasteful', as opposed to 'distasteful' human bodies. This is how capitalism, even when it is enacted by supposedly liberal minds, cannot help but inculcate and perpetuate forms of discrimination.

As the academic Eva Illouz writes in *The End of Love: A Sociology of Negative Relations* (2021): 'Sexual attractiveness mixed the sexual and the consumer in one. The visual consumer sphere, which emerged at the end of the nineteenth century, gained in extraordinary cultural and economic strength throughout the twentieth century because it made sexual identity into a visual performance mediated by consumer items.'[1] Sexual liberation, which was meant to unburden us of past tyranny and allow for the free expression of desire, was seized upon as a fresh opportunity for commerce. Through the perpetuation of the idea that only one, extremely narrow version of desirability and attractiveness existed, advertisers whipped us into a frenzy of seeking to emulate an ideal under threat of being excluded from that most basic and rewarding aspect of the human experience – connection. The vast majority of us believed that the only way to achieve the desirable look, which had been chosen, deliberately, for its anomaly status (tall and narrow yet curvaceous, athletic but effortless-seeming – at least for women) was by purchasing a variety of proxies (namely products and treatments) that promised to deliver similar results.

The prescribed standards of beauty during the earliest days of advertising were also informed by the appearances of the most powerful. The spectacle of the white, athletic model served as a sort of distant beacon, steering the overall direction of consumer desire in favour of the landowners and capitalists, but also, crucially, informing consumers that they would never be within its reach. Beauty would be dictated to us on almost every inch of printed matter and every screen throughout the Western world. But despite its ubiquity, its power rested in the perception that it was also god-given and miraculous – a quality to which we could only ever aspire and never fully attain. As a result, beauty was something that never revealed itself too plainly, in a performance that was as much about concealment and deflection, as enticement. Beauty rarely smiled or showed its gums, its movements were limited and modest. Beauty carried associations with the delicate, the ethereal and the unattainable.

Its consolation prize, then – its only son that it gave to the world – was sexiness, which was far more animated and pronounced. As Illouz writes, 'Sexiness was more democratic than beauty in that it could be achieved by a much larger pool of people.' This is 'because it is the result of self-fashioning rather than of in-born beauty, [making] consumption an ongoing and permanent feature of the experience of the self'. Sexiness, which had ostensibly come to provide us relief from the taunting spectacle of the beautiful (but which could never exist without it), was again little more than a value judgement – a way of denigrating the attempts made by lowly consumers to fulfil an ideal that was never achievable. It was a way of stigmatising hair dye and extensions, contouring and shape-wear.

If the writer, which by extending the logic that applies to the corporate professional, or anyone else commanding a degree of authority, needed to assume an air of god-given superiority in order to justify its place in the social order (one that I should stress is far more about kudos than financial remuneration in the current climate), then sexiness – which implied something synthetic and hard-won – would need to be avoided. The body of the writer would need to seem effortlessly slim, tidy and manicured, while avoiding any obvious signs of interference – similar to the body of the corporate professional, which also need to become an emblem of prosperity through its tacit communication of a lifestyle that enjoyed juice cleanses, gym memberships and personal trainers. The problem – and it was not just one problem, but an infinite number of problems in fact, whose harm would be impossible to ever calculate or measure – was that the transformation of the body into a site of consumer desire, led to the delusion that the person who happened to have, say, large breasts or a large ass, but really any physical body that was visible and self-possessed, was also in some way actively marketing itself or seeking to make itself more commercially viable to a sexualised, mass-market gaze.

In the comment that was made about my body, then, it would seem as though I was on the receiving end of these various forces, as were billions of other people the world over, though mainly women, who had also been forced to conceal or repress certain parts of themselves in the name of being taken 'seriously' and having any real stake in the professional job market; a very literal rendering of the *less is more* truism that I heard echoed in countless fashion videos that I watched in my research for this chapter. It is a phrase uttered by models whose appearances are also the result of immense effort and expenditure, and whose emulation would cost even more for the average consumer. The phrase, then, which has been in common usage for so long now as to almost sound trite, is nevertheless, and like those phrases governing tastefulness in other areas of life, about achieving a minimalism that conceals the effort of its creation. It is not about abstaining from beauty products and rituals altogether, but becoming more adept in our usage of them such that an outside observer could not detect any obvious signs or traces.

Disobedient bodies

To further illustrate the false dichotomy that has been created between ideas of natural beauty and a bought sexiness, we might consider the work of Spanish film director Pedro Almodóvar. Not since Botticelli started painting maidens in smocks wielding scabbards and the severed heads of fallen victims in the sixteenth century, has a man in the arts done so much to promote the cause of women, their safety and fulfilment. From helping to popularise ideas of trans-inclusive feminism, LGBTQIA+ equality, abortion rights and reasonable, sympathetic attitudes towards HIV and AIDS, Almodóvar's films also deal in themes that are more ambient, but no less crucial, to women's experience – themes such as beauty, but also friendship, desirability and love. Perhaps the theme of beauty is nowhere more vivid than in Almodóvar's *The Skin I Live In* (2011), a film about cosmetic surgery, in which Dr Robert Ledgard, played by Antonio Banderas, successfully transplants a new, injury-resistant strain of skin onto the body of his patient Vera, played by Elena Anaya. Suffice to say I enjoy films dealing in skin, womanhood, and identity, and that this particular film made explicit Almodóvar's own preoccupation with similar themes, which nevertheless formed a tacit focus of works made in the years prior.

My favourite Almodóvar film, *All About My Mother* (1999), is an expansive saga centred on protagonist Manuela's journey in overcoming the grief caused by a life-altering event in the film's first quarter. Manuela finds solace and new meaning through the relationships that she forms with a wide range of women living in Barcelona, each maligned by society in one way or another, but resilient and tightly bound to each other as a result. This includes several trans women, as well as a young nun, who is also HIV-positive, played by Penélope Cruz in her first major role. As an example of female solidarity and of social organising in ways that preclude patriarchal dominance, it is arguably the most famous cultural offering ever made on the subject, and as a result of these ideas coinciding with a concern for the question of beauty and how it impacts women's lives, it is a film that also helped transform my own relationship with my body and appearance.

Without sanctimony, *All About My Mother* presents a definition of beauty that has evolved outside of traditional advertising and the misogyny that it normalises, and with characters who have developed an irreverent disdain towards the conventional trappings of girlishness, femininity and quiet submissiveness to the male gaze. The casting of Penélope Cruz here is crucial, too, as her character's HIV diagnosis hastens the cruelties of a world that would otherwise valorise her youth, slimness and conformity to a traditional gender binary, demonstrating that everyone is susceptible and no one is safe, even those who might enjoy the fleeting luxury (debatable and offset by frequent predations, I might add) of what tradition maintains to be beautiful. I first watched *All About My Mother* at the BFI in London in my early twenties, where it struck me for reasons that were not just relevant to my own experience, but also, I felt, the very particular shifts in the language of beauty and advertising that were taking place all around me. If the world of the 2000s with its ghoulish demand for skinniness and poker-straight hair had created its own set of problems in the mind of the author, such that I was undernourished and in a permanent state of agitation from the age of fourteen until my early thirties, then I had at least been spared the additional worry about the judgements of artifice. What had emerged in the years since, however, was a fixation with minimal beauty interventions and natural appearances, as the same companies that had once promised to transform, alter or enhance our appearances, shifted to promising to help us reveal a beauty that ought to be innate.

Starting out as the personal blog of its founder, a woman called Emily Weiss, Glossier is now one of the world's highest grossing beauty companies. In its earlier incarnation as a blog, *Into the Gloss* had been a place for people so inclined to read about the art of achieving clear, flawless and hydrated skin. Soon Glossier would provide the very products with which to achieve those same ends, peddling a very specific and contemporary view of beauty that was all about letting the real person shine out, with gentle topical formulations to enhance shine, add a light wash of colour or create the impression of a healthy glow. Brands like this seemed to advocate a more democratic and realistic version of beauty than was popular in the decades prior, one in which all people should have the confidence to 'embrace' their 'real selves'. But the problem with this was twofold. On the one hand, old and unrealistic beauty standards had not been replaced, and Glossier still used models who broadly fit the same autocratic ideals that had existed for decades, only now instead of having the hallowed and impenetrable air of Christy Turlington on a billboard campaign in the 1990s – a spectacle which we could all largely agree on being unrealistic and out of reach – the apparent democracy of a brand like Glossier led to an assumption than the impossible beauty standard walked among us, bringing our failure to fulfil its ideals into sharper focus. On the other hand, and much more profoundly, I believe, it also perpetuated the false and harmful myth of there being a natural versus an unnatural self, negating the idea that our identities might constitute an ongoing performance and a series of habits that are constantly being re-evaluated and adjusted.

Does the routine use of multiple skincare products, certain exercises prescribed for boosting the complexion, and the conscious effort to drink over two litres of water a day, constitute something more natural than the application of heavy foundation or powder? When we question the definition of *natural* – and really try to arrive at a concrete definition of what that might mean – the idea invariably falls apart. Assuming facial fillers and Botox constitute a departure from the natural, what are the implications of cutting or dyeing one's hair, suntanning, getting orthodontic work, using hair removal methods, brushing one's teeth, clipping one's toenails, showering of a morning? The 'natural' implies that there is a state of being that is absolute and definitive. It implies that bodies are static and fixed in a particular condition. But where exactly is this natural state? What is natural, and what is not? Without being able to fix on a satisfactory definition, we reach a point of realising that natural does not denote a state of being, so much as offer a value judgement, like beauty or sexiness, that serves to either approve of, or exclude, its object. The more important question to ask ourselves is not what is beautiful or what isn't, or what is natural or what isn't, but what either word is being used to lend legitimacy to, and by reverse, denigrate and mock.

Crucial to Manuela's story in *All About My Mother* is her involvement with amateur theatre, the place in which many of her new acquaintances are forged, and a site of healing, redemption and a renewed sense of meaning, but also, crucially, a place of performance and play. As Manuela assumes understudy roles on stage, her personal life undergoes a process of reflection as she considers the alternative roles she might assume beyond just that of motherhood. These include a friend, a confidante, a cook, an actress, a teacher and a leader. Almodóvar's film is about the curative effects of performance, and the woman's agility in being able to fulfil multiple and conflicting roles in the course of a life. It is a film that pushes against the static, monofunctional image of the Madonna in passive servitude to her valuable cargo, the Christ, or the idea that woman exists in any one particular or 'naturalised' state; and this is only compounded by its inclusion of trans women, to showcase the full spectrum of experience and presentation that the rubric of 'womanhood' contains. It is a celebration of the woman's ability to endlessly metamorphosise, and how this tendency might be rehearsed and perfected through the conscious assumption of alternative roles and aliases through art, something that so many women practitioners, from Ana Mendieta to Cindy Sherman, have also explored in their work. In presenting this radical, fluid, and ultimately elusive definition of womanhood, we are also invited to see ourselves in much the same way and to consider the variety of roles and performances that we enter into both with deliberate thought, to escape ourselves and enjoy the freedom of exhibitionism and play, but also those that we enter into as a result of being alive and needing to fulfil the duties of our circumstance. All of which, the film suggests, might be a part of an act that we call the self, and which ultimately is mutable and subject to change.

Within this, too, Almodóvar makes explicit the fact that beauty, or perhaps sexiness, is another such performance – one that many of us are taught is an obligation of womanhood, and which, with any luck, we evolve to have more of a nuanced and comfortable relationship with over time. In what for me is the film's standout scene, Agrado, an old friend of Manuela's and a transgender sex worker, offers a similar thesis. Tasked in that moment with entertaining an audience at a cabaret club whose lead performers have all been forced to cancel, Agrado performs her monologue to an audience that at first seems disappointed, then bemused, then totally enthralled by its message of radical resistance of conventional beauty standards and the misogyny contained therein. Undoing a few buttons of her cardigan, and shrugging suggestively to those around her, Agrado proceeds to point in turn to the various parts of her body altered through cosmetic procedure, and in some cases harmed through physical assault. With a delicate, coquettish delivery she recites what now reads like a prose poem: 'Almond-shaped eyes, 80,000. Nose, 200,000 and a waste of money because the next year a beating left it like this. It gives me character, but if I'd known I wouldn't have touched it ... Tits, two because I'm no monster. 70,000 each, but I've more than earned that back ... A pint [of silicone] costs about 100,000. So you work it out because I've lost count. Jaw reduction, 75,000. Complete laser depilation, because women, like men, also come from apes, 60,000 a session. It depends how hairy you are. Usually two or four sessions. But if you're a flamenco diva, you'll need more.'

Agrado's speech puts forward an idea of beauty as self-actualisation; of becoming the truest and most honest version of ourselves. This is not a fixed self, but through the long journey that she takes us on in the course of her monologue, Agrado suggests that it is a self we are always seeking to better understand and engage with, through experimentations in appearances and sexuality, but also by trusting a voice inside of us that might only be heard by disengaging from, and sounding out, other external barometers of worth.

A similar sentiment was echoed by the writer and artist Nina Arsenault, when discussing a performance entitled *40 Days and 40 Nights: Working Towards a Spiritual Experience*, in which she self-flagellates in front of a mirror. As quoted by the critic Philippa Snow, Arsenault said: 'My work explores cultural constructed ideas of maleness and femaleness, realness and fakeness ... My ideas about objectifying myself are not even my ideas, and they're not even new ideas. They are everywhere in culture. I've objectified myself in numerous ways. I have had cosmetic surgery, where I have taken the idea that I have a soul, and then I've put that on a shelf for a while and looked at my body in terms of line, form, mass and structure. And I also have an inanimate substance inside my body – silicone – so literally, there are parts of me that are inanimate, and yet they're me.' Discussing Arsenault's subsequent admission that there is 'a lot of drama and theatre involved' in being a woman, Snow suggests that, 'Arsenault's transition into something *more than* – ultra-sexual, hugely buxom, her teal eyes and pillowy, heart-shaped mouth conspiring with her unreal figure to suggest either a femmebot or a souped-up mannequin of Paris Hilton – is not meant to be read as the natural outcome of a gender reassignment, but as three-dimensional, conceptual commentary on the nature of the feminine itself.'[2]

If Arsenault suggests that the soul be parked in the construction of the body and its outer appearance, then Agrado's speech differs slightly in suggesting that through such adjustments the soul may become manifest and externalised.

Agrado's speech ends, 'Well, as I was saying, it costs a lot to be authentic, ma'am. And one can't be stingy with these things because you are more authentic the more you resemble what you've dreamed of being.' It remains a perfect riposte to the traditions of the Hollywood dream machine, which had always fought hard to conceal the lengths that its stars must go to in order to survive it. The scene is now so famous that it would seem to offer us few opportunities for fresh insight. And yet in all the analyses I have read, none seem to focus on its deliberate subversion of a form that is absolutely central to the Western literary tradition.

The exquisite corpse

Drawing elaborate metaphors between a woman's body and grandiose phenomena, usually occurring elsewhere in the natural world, to emphasise the enormity of the speaker's desire, is a poetic device that is originally attributed to the Italian Renaissance poet, Petrarch. Petrarch's eponymous conceit was popular in the literary circles of sixteenth- and seventeenth-century Europe, among them John Donne and William Shakespeare, the latter of which famously used the device in the well-quoted Sonnet 18, which begins: 'Shall I compare thee to a summer's day?' But there are countless instances from both poets, and many of their contemporaries, reaching for objects or geographical phenomena with which to analogise the female form. It is here however, that the reduction of women's bodies to a sort of catalogue – and the form lampooned in Agrado's speech – seems to have been encoded in the culture, and it also went some way to creating the impression of the woman as a sedentary being whose beauty needed to be in-born and discoverable by the male artist viewer.

In the centuries that followed, demand for portraits of reclining nudes continued the analogy between the body and multiple hillocks, streams and bushes. These images were replicated endlessly throughout the early modern period, but most notably in the depictions of Venus created by Titian, Giorgione and others, in which the woman's body would often be placed against a backdrop of undulating hills. Paintings such as the *Dresden Venus* (Giorgione) situated the reclining female nude against so much background detail, that to absorb the painting in its entirety required the viewer to scan the length of the body slowly rather than as a whole, taking in each part in turn. The word cinematic is anachronistic, and too strong for describing the encounter that contemporary audiences would have had with these works, but the urge to conceive of the body in a compartmentalised way, similar perhaps to a series of disparate 'shots', would have been unavoidable. Nevertheless, it was only with the help of the movie camera that this formula was finally able to realise its full potential.

If the static image provided a snapshot that the eye was free to peruse at leisure, then the moving image often instructed our gaze more directly. By the early twentieth century the woman would finally be afforded some movement, but never as much as her male counterparts. If Buster Keaton and Charlie Chaplin showcased the freedom of movement created by the movie camera, ushering in a chaos and a bombast, then female silent movie actresses of equivalent fame behaved much more like partially animated paintings, celebrated not for their flailing limbs and unpredictable gestures, but their otherworldliness, distant, far-off expressions and arresting stares. Helpfully, crass nicknames attributed to women actors of the time provide an insight into their objectification and the ways in which they were variously reduced to one or several physical attributes: Mary Pickford, or 'the Girl with the Curls', Jean Harlow, or 'the Blonde Bombshell', Louise Brooks, or 'the Girl in the Black Helmet', Lana Turner or 'the Sweater Girl', and Constance Talmadge, or 'Dutch' on account of her faintly northern-European appearance. It is why actresses like Bette Davis stood out among their peers, eventually appearing on screen and presenting an erratic and complex femininity, whose large eyes, traditionally tasked with delivering a dolefulness, railed against their categorisation to convey rage, joviality and good humour; but which above all else, strove, as though it were their sole aim, against any notion of the woman as a passive entity – pretty and still.

Yet despite the efforts of Davis to inject film programming with a spirited femininity, Hollywood stereotypes persisted. Perhaps the most obvious enactment of the industry's stubborn misogyny was in a device that referenced the Petrarchan conceit and that soon became a tired cliché, of the camera panning the length of a woman's body slowly. This usually started at the feet, for maximum suspense, then moved gradually up the length of the woman's legs, lingering over her torso, her breasts and her collarbone, before finally lighting on the one feature that would lend her any degree of agency or character: her face. So frequently has this motif been used, it would require more space than I have here to list all its examples, but notable among these are the final scene and post-makeover reveal of Sandy in *Grease* (1978) and the reveal of Lisa in *Weird Science* (1985). There is a slight variation on this, where the woman is afforded just a fraction more movement, albeit not much, as she descends the stairs or otherwise saunters past her new admirers. Director Billy Wilder uses such a motif when introducing the seductive Phyllis Dietrichson in *Double Indemnity* (1944), played by Barbara Stanwyck, but it is replicated time and time again in similar reveal scenes from *She's All That* (1999), and parodied in the *Naked Gun* films (1988–94), as well as the post-makeover reveal of Cady Heron, played by Lindsay Lohan, in *Mean Girls* (2004).

It was not until Ursula Andress's reveal from the waters in the James Bond film *Dr. No* (1962), where she is exposed in reverse (that is, by the head and with the upper body showcased first), that we observed any real innovation in the form, and one that beyond hinting at a slightly more empowered femininity – the bikini Andress wears contains a military belt complete with scabbard for carrying a large knife – hardly did much to hasten women's liberation on screen. This reveal is such a stock piece of footage and so cartoonish in its titillation as to even be lampooned by children's films, whose target audiences are already so indoctrinated to its absurd objectification of women that they can easily understand the joke: films such as *Who Framed Roger Rabbit* (1988) and *The Mask* (1994), where Cameron Diaz's entrance echoes the earlier burlesque performance by Roger Rabbit's cartoon wife, Jessica. The device was eventually also lampooned by the Bond franchise itself, in the 2006 film *Casino Royale*, when director Martin Campbell chose to invert the gaze and have Bond himself, played by Daniel Craig, emerge from the water in a seductive fashion.

The one instance from film history that stands out vividly when discussing this motif, and which seems most relevant for comparison with Agrado's speech however, is that of Marilyn Monroe on a train station platform in *Some Like It Hot* (1959), again directed by Billy Wilder. In its stylistic dimensions, this scene might only be considered a distant cousin of the others, being as it is a dolly shot in which the span of the woman's figure is cut short. It is also not the first time we see Marilyn, who has already been revealed to us moments earlier when she walks towards Joe, played by Tony Curtis, and Jerry, played by Jack Lemmon, both dressed as women for the purposes of trying to escape New York City unnoticed. The pair are transfixed by the performatively distracted, totally self-absorbed glamour of her character, Sugar Kane, as she saunters past them, legs radiant in a pair of seamed stockings peeping out from under a heavy, fur-trimmed coat.

As she dodges a plume of steam escaping one of the carriages (an image that carries echoes of the young Anna Karenina at the beginning of her own story, and a poignant one given the circumstances of Marilyn's own death), the performance is interrupted, and somewhat disrupted and exposed, by the blunt instruments of modernity and practical, everyday life. The train platform is a useful tool for storytellers, being a site of so many first and last encounters, but it is also one in which we are all reduced to spectacle and observer – a place where we become dislocated from circumstance and reduced to bodies in transit, our stories concealed and made somewhat irrelevant.

The response from the two admirers is interesting. Jerry, played by Jack Lemmon, seems incredulous. 'Look at that,' he says, transfixed by the spectacle of femininity that he is unable to emulate himself. 'Look at how she moves. That's just like Jell-O on springs. It must have some kind of built-in motor or something. I'm telling you, it's a whole other sex.'

'What are you afraid of?' Joe asks. 'Nobody's asking you to have a baby.'

In Jerry's response, the female subject shifts from sentient being in control of her own desirability, to passive object available for consumption: the journey from 'she' to 'that' to 'it'. Jerry is initially willing to accept that the woman is the author of her own sexuality, but as he struggles to reconcile this with his own limitations in being able to embody the same power and appeal, his generosity subsides, and the virtue necessarily become something that must be innate: *I'm telling you, it's a whole other sex.*

What's especially ironic about this outdated and reductive joke in hindsight, is how much we know of Marilyn's performance as a sex symbol, and how many books, documentaries and fictionalised retellings have been dedicated to its exploration. It was a performance that was able to satisfy the greedy appetite of the American media more successfully than any other attempt made since, but which also required elaborate makeup, shapewear, surgical procedures and a concerted adjustment of manners and speech. With Marilyn, it is never easy to make a distinction between the performer and the person – in fact, she makes the case for there being no such distinction at all, in reality, for any of us – the former having been so deliberate, and so distinct a fictional construct from the pre-fame Norma Jean, that the tabloid life and public appearances outside of the clearly demarcated theatre or cinema screen must also be considered a facet of her artistry. It is hardly derogatory to say then, that oftentimes it was not the actress, so much as the persona, who was cast in certain roles. And that it was maybe Marilyn – the performance that was given to the movie camera that never stopped rolling, even beyond the studio lot – which, far and above any individual performance by a single actor for a single role, constituted the great star turn of the twentieth century.

The casting of Monroe in *Some Like it Hot* is a stroke of genius for this reason, and she brings a level of high camp unthinkable from any of her contemporaries, none of whom ever seemed quite so in on the joke of their own celebrity, nor so ready to parody themselves. *Some Like It Hot* is about the necessity of performance in surviving modern America, as each character affects a persona to escape, either by fleeing the state and evading the attention of the authorities while wearing a disguise, or improving their situation through marriage, and the seduction of a rich man. Much like the Almodóvar film made forty years later, *Some Like It Hot* made explicit the artifice that is a condition of modern societies built on the idea of individualism, where each of us must resort to whatever means necessary in order to survive. Yet in Jerry's speech, we witness the ways in which that genius of performance, when it is a performance of womanhood, is often downplayed and denied by patriarchal assumptions, who feel it would be too generous to the woman's intellect and wiles to admit that they had been duped by whatever role she was affecting: the 'she' to 'that' to 'it' methodology by which the act of beauty and gender had been dismissed for centuries and furiously attributed to some 'natural' state of womanhood that is elusive and only possessed by the chosen few.

'All I have that's real,' says Agrado, 'are my feelings and these pints of silicone that weigh a ton.' Almodóvar could have had his character deliver a sob story or a diatribe, railing against the harms done to her and the discrimination that she has faced. Doing this, however, would only have reinforced the idea of Agrado's difference, of her being somehow divergent from a norm on account of the gender-reaffirming procedures that she had undergone. Instead, by choosing to have her adopt the same narrative technique employed by men for centuries – the cold, unfeeling survey of various features, each considered in turn and distinct from the other – Almodóvar makes the viewer, which in this case consists both of the audience within the film and those of us without, complicit: who of you out there have not been titillated by a woman's body presented in the manner of a price card, itemised and categorised according to individual attributes? But also, who of you alive in this system of individual ambition and competition, where we are all debased and forced to sell ourselves in whatever ways are available to us, have not satisfied the male gaze through slight but continual adjustments in your appearance, and in exchange for the benefits that it might confer?

There is no judgement implied here, but the opposite. There is an appeal for the viewer to desist in their judgements of people who only make more explicit, and obvious, the tendencies of all of us. Agrado's efforts are notable for being in service of something much more self-fulfilling and admirable however, than the simple, reflexive fulfilment of roles designated at birth that we see in the behaviours of those who are dutifully and frantically performing a type of cis-gendered normativity.

Agrado's speech is, of course, a powerful statement on the nature of identity, legitimising the experience of trans and non-binary people and asserting their equal place in a society where it has been historically maligned. But more fundamentally, it is about positing an alternative definition of natural beauty, from the conditions of someone's birth to the expression of a self that is defined elsewhere: of Dolly Parton identifying with the image of the woman that she had witnessed in the grocery store, whom her mother, and the rest of the neighbourhood, had scorned, and who she determined to spend the rest of her life emulating. It is the image of Pamela Anderson calling out to me with a generosity that seemed to be lacking elsewhere in pop culture; the freedom symbolised by her large bouffant hair, spider-leg eyebrows, horned eyeshadow and frosted lips, wielding a gun in the video store in Birmingham, where working people were always being told to conceal their desires and conform to a set of autocratic rules decided by those in power. It was an image that admitted to me, as it did to the entire world, that Anderson was not too proud, nor too ashamed, to make explicit her sexuality and desire; a symbol of an enlarged femininity, if you like, but also a somewhat subverted femininity, refusing the idea that she should demure and make herself small, and exaggerating her proportions instead through implants, stilettos and back-combed hair. Because the end point of our society's fixation with so-called natural beauty would be total inertia, which is the point. It is the reduction of woman to object, where she is still, lifeless and unthreatening, but also where her worth and viability are assessed according to some external metric, as opposed to something gained through self-invention.

After watching *All About My Mother*, and in the years that I was struggling to contend with my own insecurities of appearance, I was struck by what seemed to be a growing puritanism with respect to the performances of cis-gendered people, as an almost psychotic fixation emerged over who might require the least interference in order to be considered viable, and beautiful. This dynamic also pitted itself in opposition to more maximalist styles that had been popularised by queer communities, and particularly the ballroom scenes, in major cities.

'Natural' vs 'exotic'

Natural beauty also precludes and subtly castigates ideas that have evolved outside of the Western tradition, such as in Bollywood with its frequent use of kohl eyeliner, sparkly eyeshadows and velvet-painted crimson lips. What, on the face of it then, presents as an effort to liberate people from the lengthy and laborious makeup routines that many actually enjoy (!), also fails to recognise its opposition to a variety of cultural strains that sit outside the broadly white, Western standard. It might seem odd to have cited so many examples from the golden age of Hollywood in this chapter, yet being the place where so many ideas of beauty were first established, or at least popularised in Western culture, its realities might not be so far as we imagine from our own. The treatment by studio bosses and the media of so many Hollywood movie stars, Marilyn included, was barbaric, but while much of what happened to these women has been nominally censured in the contemporary entertainment industry, its residual effects can still be felt.

The first Hollywood movie star who ever captured my imagination was Merle Oberon, playing Catherine Earnshaw alongside Laurence Olivier as Heathcliff, in the 1939 film adaptation of *Wuthering Heights*. It was a film that my mother loved, particularly the scene in which Heathcliff carries Catherine's limp body to the window of the Earnshaw residence so that they can look upon the moors together one final time. This film was played so often in our house and its emotional impact on my mother left such an indelible mark, that it created a lifelong love in me for the Emily Brontë novel, this particular adaptation, and Merle's performance above all else, which leant Catherine's tainted experience of social mobility an air of frenzy.

Oberon passed away in 1979 and has never been a popular, household name. This made it more surprising when she was mentioned in connection with Michelle Yeoh's nomination for Best Actress at the 2023 Academy Awards, for her performance in the film *Everything Everywhere All at Once* (2022). *Hollywood Reporter* claimed that Yeoh was 'the first person who identifies as Asian to ever be nominated for the award', prompting many journalists and commentators to point out that that achievement had in fact been Oberon's when she was nominated for her role in the *The Dark Angel* (1935). Yet owing to a complex and tragic story involving the concealment of her race and upbringing, most audiences, myself included, had always assumed that Oberon was white.

In the film adaptation of *Wuthering Heights* (1939), Merle is a ghostly figure whose pale complexion is only heightened by the contrast with her very dark hair. The pallor was so extreme that it seemed plausible to me as a child that she could have been an apparition. Yet Oberon was born with dark skin and was the daughter of a British man and a Sri Lankan woman – there is some dispute as to whether she was in fact mothered by the woman who claimed to be her sister, who was nevertheless also a Sri Lankan woman. What is certain is that Oberon was born Estelle Merle O'Brien Thompson in Calcutta, where she later became a party girl and was a regular at many of the city's nightclubs, developing a network of contacts that allowed her to forge an acting career in Britain, America and beyond.

That Oberon was initially marketed as a white actress was a business decision made in a world that was still explicitly racist. It was an illusion that she was able to maintain through heavy makeup and skin-whitening treatments that would prove to have long-term negative health effects. These included skin bleaching and supplements, which compromised Oberon's immune system and brought about various allergic reactions that permanently altered the state of her skin. The whitening was also accompanied by an elaborate web of lies that Oberon was tasked with maintaining both to contacts in the industry and in interviews. In many profiles she is recorded as saying that she had been born and raised in Tasmania.

The effect of sulfa drugs to whiten the skin eventually led to an allergic reaction that caused Oberon to suffer permanent facial disfigurement that was only partially corrected by continual dermabrasion procedures. Oberon spent much of her career masking the harm caused by skin bleaching and supplements, and developed many strategies for concealing its effects from the camera. The pale figure that we see in *Wuthering Heights* then, is partly an illusion created by lighting techniques that were developed especially for Oberon, but also several layers of concealer and powder – products that had once been used to mask her natural skin colour, that were now being used to mask the effects of trying to erase that skin colour altogether.

At the height of her career, however, and in the midst of all this activity to alter her appearance, Oberon nevertheless appeared in several print advertisements for the cosmetics company Max Factor, and one in particular promoting a lip palette that read, 'Far more lovely – since she began to reveal her natural charm. Merle Oberon ... before, the slightly unreal exotic, now the beautiful, natural, charming girl.'[3] The explicit racism of this ad was nothing unusual in the advertising of 1930s America. What is somewhat striking, however, is the way in which this ad uses 'natural' synonymously with 'white'. Even allowing for the ignorance of marketeers and audiences as to Merle's actual heritage, it suggested that her 'true' identity could only be 'revealed' through the application of products that allowed her skin to appear paler. This is not the self-created identity referred to by Agrado, but one decided by and forcefully imposed by society and which favoured middle-class white women; and by reverse, exoticised and denigrated anyone who was not. There is also the insinuation that the 'exotic' (a racist term used to make an oddity of people who are not white) also meant licentious and illicit. We would see this stereotype played out repeatedly, in long dark-haired temptresses disrupting the otherwise civilised order presided over by the 'beautiful, naturally charming' (read: blonde) 'girl' in cinema and elsewhere in pop culture.

Oberon's story might seem somewhat niche and out of time, but it speaks to a culture that was never wholly corrected, and her example allows us to consider the harms that that word 'natural' still carries, and at a time when its currency has never been so high. In the current demands for clear, translucent and unblemished skin, are echoes of a trend displayed vividly in artworks such as the Armada Portrait of Queen Elizabeth I (unattributed), but also fashions of the sixteenth, seventeeth and eighteenth centuries in which wealthy landowners and royalty would frequently enhance the whiteness of their skin through powder, and manually apply blue paint to the temples and throat to create the appearance of veins. Later in the Victorian period, it was not uncommon for middle-class women seeking to affect the appearance of wealth, to bathe themselves in arsenic, a practice that led to countless injuries and fatalities. This was all done to create the appearance of having never needed to work outside, be exposed to the sun, or toil for endless hours in a way that might lead to a toughening of the skin over time. In almost every element of Queen Elizabeth I's attire, for example, is the demonstration of impracticality – from the vast, weighty garments worn over her person, with their intricate detailing and thousands of woven jewels, to the perma-set hair in its gravity-defying fashion. It is a look that says: *I will gather and display the spoils of my kingdom, without having any practical role in their creation.* Or for example, Marie Antoinette, whose childhood portraits show a figure that is sheet white and almost farcical in the petiteness of her nose and mouth, and in the exaggeratedly large proportions of her eyes; who in adult life would be shown to the public in hairstyles amounting to the frosting of a cake that she famously taunted the people of France with, frothing over in vast powdered tendrils interspersed with feathers and pearls.

Today's affluent beauty influencers might not choose to express themselves in quite the same manner, but in promoting a beauty standard that is all about purity of complexion, a regular exercise regime and a diet of exclusively cold-press juices, there is nevertheless an attempt to convey the privileges of a cosseted lifestyle. This is also present in beauty trends urging us to achieve a certain iridescence and dewiness of skin texture, when it is enough for most working people to keep the sweat at bay long enough to seem vaguely composed.

All of which might seem obvious, but we nevertheless marvel at the flagrant inequality on display in regal portraiture of the past, and in the horrifying standards of the antiquated Hollywood machine, and yet satisfy ourselves with the assumptions of progress. Yet while the idioms have shifted – the styles changed, along with the vocabulary, the brand names and the diet fads – many of the dynamics highlighted here have proven to be remarkably stubborn and unable to be separated from activity in the present day. What's more, a vigilance is required in thinking about certain words, and not just 'natural' or indeed 'simple', but also in the language of luminescence that is so common to the modern beauty industry, with all its implied judgements about the preference for that which is 'light' or 'bright'.

Quite simply, while beauty standards might seem to have been democratised, on account of almost anyone being able to broadcast via social media, their discussion has become that much harder to escape and the opportunity for change, radically reduced on account of an algorithm that generally favours familiarity and pre-existing 'norms'. Archetypes of the past might have been more rigid and unachievable, but as stated, they were at least consigned to a magazine that might be closed or thrown away, or a TV screen that we at least had the willpower to switch off. If body dysmorphia and disordered eating are often born of a tendency that is linked with obsessive compulsive disorder, of simply being unable to think about anything else, then the constant availability of images and discussion related to images facilitated by today's technology, presents a maddening dilemma.

What's more, the hazard of 'harmful beauty standards', as the media puts it, is one of the preoccupations of the age, and with good reason: op-eds and online debates as to the damage being caused by social media filters, weight-loss aids and invasive procedures highlight the adverse effect of our visual culture on those who identify as women in particular. But as with multiple phenomena subject to the face-value scrutiny of a facile journalism, this commentary is often also guilty of reinforcing a naturalised view of beauty – of beauty as fact. It perpetuates the erroneous belief that a beauty ideal is anything other than a set of standards agreed by a minority of media workers themselves, as well as advertisers, to perpetuate consumer desire and the current order of power, and that it is only corrosive on account of the pressure that is felt by individuals in trying to conform to it. The media often concedes that beauty is changeable, and particularly during the 2000s, when a fairly hostile fixation on the 'size zero' body set in, it was common for comparisons to be drawn with the beauty standards of the 1950s, where women had been celebrated for their 'curves'. Yet these facts are always wielded as proof of a beauty standard that has gone awry, or deviated from a more 'healthy' and 'natural' starting point, rather than to demonstrate the fundamentally illusory nature of beauty, or 'sexiness', as they are commonly defined. If we were to find another, more accurate term, divorced from the swell of affection and desire that we feel towards another person – which is never really about physical appearances, and when it is, arguably only as a result of a societal tendency to over-emphasise the importance of the visual – then it might be used to more clearly indicate the aesthetic judgements that are decided at the social level, and which rest upon all of the bigotries and cruelties contained within that society as a result.

The appearance of power

Our impression of how a person looks can also be completely tied to the way that we feel about them, and this in itself disproves whatever standard might exist. Just as we find beauty in a person when they present as friendly, affectionate and interested – and vice versa – we are just as susceptible to the marketing of certain individuals as sex symbols. We can never really extract our own judgements from those that we have been coaxed into having by the psychological manipulation of the advertiser. What if the real harm was not merely in the stipulations of a given standard at a given time, but in labouring under the idea that physical beauty, divorced from feeling, exists at all, and is not instead a fallacy equivalent to, say race, nationality or gender?

Rather than seeking to remedy our pain by liberalising the beauty standard that currently exists to include a wider scope of body shapes and skin types (which in their assertion as 'beautiful' must always necessarily create an opposite: an ugly, a deficient, a deformed), what if we were to distrust any notion of physical beauty altogether? After all, the sensation of being attracted to someone outside the bounds of what we might deem acceptable among our friends or wider society, is one of the great predicaments of the dating age, whose apps facilitate a tendency to avoid dating in the cold light of day those same people who are nevertheless capable of inducing us to climax in the tepid gloom of evening. And is this not a form of insanity?

Of course, it is with possible good reason that the relationship between beauty, power and politics is rarely discussed: an association between the three was harnessed by despots in some of the worst crimes ever committed in human history. But those crimes were only possible due to the false but nevertheless pervasive view that beauty is innate. When we fail to see beauty as a projection of the powerful and the product of oppression, we are susceptible to it being used as grounds to further that oppression. Dictators often turn matters of history into conspiracy: that white people have been the more powerful for centuries is unquestionable, but that power was only as a result of the fortuitous oppression of other people. White supremacism ignores that history, to suggest that an inherent distinction has now come under threat. Beauty – in the formal, purely aesthetic sense of the word – often forms part of a process of naturalisation, and the illusion of an inherent superiority and the fated dominance of one group of people over another. We might shy away from the topic for fear of causing offence or unleashing some terrible pattern of events into the world, but our caution is misguided, and any anti-fascist cause that is only prepared to tackle surface level phenomena, rather than seeking to understand its subliminal presence in thought patterns that each and every one of us is susceptible to having, is one that is fundamentally unserious.

For years I avoided writing about beauty, judging it to be facile and beneath me. This was an act of internalised misogyny, as cruel in its censure of my interests and worries as the harsh words about my appearance and appetites that boyfriends had made over the years. In fact, I would go so far as to say that I often shaped my interests to please the people I was dating; seeking to make my intellectual repertoire an extension of my beauty, or to compensate for the failure of my physical appearance by constructing an image that would allow me to fulfil some other type that was perhaps bookish, studious or creative. Ultimately, however, an interest in aesthetics and politics and the harsh, unhealthy judgements that occur between people who have more to gain through liking each other, cannot afford to overlook the subject of beauty.

I realise, too, by distrusting the existence of physical

beauty in any real aesthetic sense, I am also desecrating one of the last vestiges of sublime sentiment to exist, and which many of us rely on for the purposes of finding meaning in our lives. This might not be in the belief in beauty *per se*, but in romance, which in its popular sense depends on a notion of beauty. It is so automatic, we can hardly be held responsible for it: the need to ascribe our feelings to some physical, tangible attribute, to tell this person and ourselves that they are the most beautiful thing we have ever seen. We know on a logical level that beauty is subject to social and political forces, because we feel our attractions change at different times and under different circumstances, but our commitment to a version of romance promoted by Hollywood and which centres on beauty, has a way of taking over. In a sense, beauty is almost a metaphor for attraction, and we have started to confuse the symbol for the object: we say that someone is the most beautiful person we have ever seen because we love them, and in a visually saturated culture that places appearances above anything else, few things could be more flattering. But then there emerges a necessity to make it so, to believe it, and to do whatever we can to silence the doubt that exists inside of us.

This creates a dissonance that makes attraction remarkably fragile, and I believe that it is contributing to a widespread crisis of sexuality and love. By refusing to acknowledge the wider social and cultural forces shaping our initial, visual attractions, for fear that they might shatter an illusion, and insisting instead on attributing everything to a romantic ideal with 'beauty' situated at its centre, we also, by reverse, end up translating the highly fallible and cruel assumptions of capital into absolute truths. When superficial demonstrations of cultural capital give way and the real person is discoverable to us – that is, the point at which real attraction between two people might actually begin – we are suddenly alerted to the artifice of the former, and repulsed at the possibility of having been deceived.

We see this play out in the 'ick', a term popularised by the British television show *Love Island* which refers to those quirks of personal presentation that have the power to completely turn another person off. Among icks I have seen listed online are 'the moment the barber swivels him around on the chair to reveal the back of his head'; 'when his feet don't meet the floor on a bar stool'; 'when he asks to see the soup of the day'; 'when he sticks his tongue out while reversing'; 'when he walks back after completing his turn at bowling'; 'when the bow of his shoelaces is a little too big'; 'when he uses his laptop on his lap'; 'when he wears a rucksack'; 'when he carries an umbrella'. We joke, but the concept of the ick extends to sweat in the wrong places, bogeys that are unattended to, spit in the corner of the mouth, the lingering smell of garlic on the breath, the wrong style of shoe, or slightly unexpected occurrences of body hair. Rather than being honest with ourselves from the start about the fact that this is merely another person, and that our attraction to them, while real, is based on a set of experiences and cultural codes that we have internalised, we hold someone up in an idealised way such that any deviance can suddenly, and often irrevocably, spell repulsion.

What is interesting is that our attractions seem to have become far more neurotic and liable to being destroyed at the slightest inconvenience, surprise or divergence from a very strict set of visual, or at least aesthetic, criteria. And while icks might be discussed hypothetically and for a laugh online, they nevertheless form part of a culture in which ghosting is rife and many struggle to form longstanding and constant attachments. The reason is our investment in an abstract notion of attractiveness, which as discussed previously, has to be understood as absolute and beyond reproach for us to invest in it.

This undoes the work of many writers and thinkers, in trying to explain to us that beauty, as it relates to the purely visual, is inextricable from power: that it is socially defined and always in service of supporting the incumbent keepers of wealth and power, as defined by Ruskin. It is almost as if, once we came to accept that conventional notions and standards of beauty were inextricable from questions of power, we decided not to negotiate with this reality and seek to develop rational, sane ways of ensuring that another, more sympathetic and emotional definition of beauty could coexist. Instead, we sought to reject the very idea, by insisting that beauty was, in fact, innate, mystical or a quirk of nature administered by Cupid, whose forces we could never question, and would therefore be powerless to resist.

On top of this, there is a common acceptance that beauty lends a person a degree of power: 'pretty privilege' is a term used by younger generations to refer to a person's ability to gain certain advantages on account of their looks. But what if this way of explaining the world misses the point entirely? What if it is more useful to consider beauty an extension of power, whose definition by current and popular standards was little more than an expression of the forces that rule and dominate? What if it were the case that we often only find certain people physically beautiful on account of the tacit signifiers of wealth, health, strength and dominance that they contain – and that beauty without any concept of power would look very different to how it is conceived by our media?

From one day to the next, and depending on my mood, I appear radically different to myself. Body dysmorphia is rife. Ideas of beauty cannot be trusted. In my experience too, nothing could be further from the truth than the famous adage, erroneously attributed first to Kate Moss but actually made popular by anorexia sites around 2003, that 'nothing tastes as good as skinny feels'.[4] It was the Romantics of the late eighteenth and early nineteenth centuries who identified that beauty is less an empirical observation, than a feeling – what they termed 'the sublime'. While the connection with a nineties supermodel might be opaque, learning about the sublime when I was younger put me on to the fact that, as well as beauty being able to inspire a sense of wonder, the reverse might also be true – a sense of wonder, or happiness, might also open us up to the multiple and diverse forms of beauty that exist all around us. There is often no quicker route to wonder and happiness than through the mouth, I believe, and the truth that diet slimming aids want no one to realise is that perhaps being well-fed leads to a feeling of contentment from which the entire world seems more beautiful, including the person staring back at us in the mirror.

Chapter Five

Food

Good, Honest, Simple

UNKNOWN

A few years ago while trying to make ends meet in London, and after I had quit the publishing gig only to enter the arguably worse world of freelancing, I took a job writing advertising copy for a drinks company whose main product was a series of pre-packaged juice 'cleanses'. These consisted of multiple juice products delivered in a box and intended to be consumed over the course of several days as part of a specially designed programme aimed at delivering multiple health benefits, including the spurious 'flushing out of one's system'. Never, in the few weeks that I worked for this company, was the fact of weight loss mentioned. This was the unspoken truth of the company that we were always seeking to avoid explicit mention of, and no one more so than the hired copy-writer whose job it was to name the various juice cleanses and their individual products, as well as create slogans to be pasted alongside them on boxes and in supermarkets. For several weeks I scratched my chin and wracked my brains over novel ways to convey the minimal calorie intake without ever being so explicit as to say this outright. A worthy use of my time, I think we can all agree, and one that resulted in very little besides me being swiftly replaced by a bullish ad person.

What struck me about this experience was the new language that had emerged with respect to food. In every discussion I had with the founder of this company, there was an automatic and defensive rejection of the very thing that we both knew to be true: that the company had created a new diet product, and that the founder, an enthusiastic runner and advocate of a low-carb, low-sugar diet, was in the business of selling to rich people convenient ways of dropping a few pounds. Instead, what we spoke about were the various emotional, spiritual and even pseudo-intellectual benefits of replacing every meal with a cold-pressed juice. Words such as 'joy', 'clarity', but also 'achievement', 'gratification' and 'fulfilment' were thrown around casually. Where we were prevented from being honest about what we were selling to consumers, we defaulted to a moral argument about treating the body *right*, through a programme of abstinence and restraint. The cleanliness referred to in the product's name implied the existence of an opposite: dirt. Dirty eaters would seem to constitute the people who were unable to pursue a days-long juice cleanse costing several hundred pounds a turn.

Elsewhere, a similar set of terms were being used to justify the sale of organic food products and books advocating home cooking. Not long after this experience in the halls of the juice-cleanse headquarters, I found myself on the West Coast of America, where the extremes of a food industry masquerading under the guise of a new moral system were in full effect. In a moment of desperation before going to interview an author, I dipped into a Whole Foods branch where a salad that I 'built' myself from the 'bar' whose sign promised to provide me with a home-cooked meal cost $17. Since that experience I have discovered the online world of Whole Food salad hacks, in which consumers share tips on how to avoid making 'dumb' (expensive) salads, as opposed to 'smart' (cheap) salads, the essence being that one should not purchase much ('Do not get hard-boiled eggs'; 'Skimp on beans'; 'Be mindful of the marinade' suggests one *Huffington Post* article).[1] To dwell on Whole Foods for any length of time is futile, and I am hardly going to be able to share much here that has not already been said a thousand times before about the Amazon-owned food chain. Only it is interesting perhaps to consider the name itself and the implication that anything outside of its hallowed walls constitutes an incomplete food offering. The term 'whole foods' admittedly has a life beyond the chain, and is used to refer to any food that does not contain artificial ingredients or has not been farmed and manufactured under large-scale industrial conditions. Organic food, however, is a less value-laden term, and one that does not at least imply deficiency in the foodstuffs that billions of people are forced to eat out of imposed scarcity and hardship.

As a point of contrast and what might serve as a perfect fable of the competing definitions between an outdated and more impoverished view of luxury – as something fun,

excessive and convenient, versus the rarefied and elite definition of asceticism and restraint – a day after the Whole Foods
incident I flew to Las Vegas for a two-day trip motivated
more out of curiosity than a desire to expose my nervous
system to its relentless bright lights and loud noises. In the
restaurant of the hotel New York, New York, famous for
its facade replicating the New York skyline (complete with
miniature Statue of Liberty, Chrysler Building and Empire
State Building, not to mention a full-scale roller-coaster), I
ordered an eggs benedict. This arrived in a state that would
already be questionable in the minds of a purist for its two
thick slices of cut ham that had been used instead of bacon.
But what really stole the breath and dazzled the eyes was the
inclusion, nestled between the usual two halves of an English
muffin, of a shop-bought, paper-on, overflowing chocolate
American muffin, about which pooled the thick golden lava
of a hollandaise sauce.

Nothing could have been further from the spartan world
cultivated by the juice company I had just escaped. This perverse culinary voyage I had unwittingly embarked on raised
several questions about the role played by food in all of our
lives and the tendency for it to also attract harsher judgements and moral aspersions than perhaps any other facet of
modern life.

The symbol of spaghetti

We see this play out endlessly in TV programming devoted
to the subject of health and diet. But to help convey the
subtlety with which prejudices in food culture often exert

themselves, is an example from a film exploring sexual awakening, queer identity and first love. *Blue is the Warmest Colour* (dir., Abdellatif Kechiche, 2013) is also a film about class, and how inequalities of wealth and opportunity bear out in the most mundane interactions between two people who are intimately involved and living at close quarters. Food is identified as a key site of tension, with Kechiche using its preparation and consumption to create some of the film's most memorable scenes.

Blue is centred on the relationship between two women – Adele, played by Adèle Exarchopoulos, and Emma, played by Lea Seydoux. Adele is both younger and less privileged than Emma, and this is critical to their story, shaping the relationship in ways that both characters seem powerless to control. After passing each other first on the street, and then meeting at a queer bar later by accident, theirs is a story of fortuitous love that is constantly having to grapple with the far more mercenary forces that exist all around it, including matters of careerism, work and professional identity. As anyone who has fallen in love under similar circumstances can attest, in this world of increased financial strain and human commodity value, differences of socioeconomic reality can prove insurmountable. Without compatibility of bank accounts and aspirations, a chance romance based on feelings alone, and with the added complication of homophobia to contend with, stands little chance of survival. This is the central predicament that both characters come to terms with in the course of the film.

Almost like touchstones, marking the relationship at various stages, are pivotal scenes involving either one or both women navigating meals. These occur prior to, during and in the aftermath of their time as a couple, and in almost every case involve the serving of pasta, or to be more precise, spaghetti – usually laced in a thick tomato-y sauce, and so satisfying to look upon and imagine oneself eating that the emotional chord being struck at any given time becomes all the more exaggerated and intense. Pasta being such a commonplace food, it carries for each of us a wealth of associated memories and feelings that Kechiche uses. It is this, as well as the various socioeconomic readings that might be applied to a bowl of pasta, rather than the far more common reading of its use in the film as a metaphor for sexual appetite and even cunnilingus, that interests me.[2] Crude and reductive and borne of blunt stereotypes about female desire and sexuality, these readings fail to account for the much more subtle symbolism, its commentary on class differences and the implications for our understanding of taste and power. In this way, I believe it differs dramatically from another famous instance of food on screen, and from a film that has naturally drawn comparisons with Kechiche's picture.

In *Call Me By Your Name* (dir., Luca Guadagnino, 2017), another film about sexual awakening, queer identity and first love, Elio, played by Timothée Chalamet, and Oliver, played by Armie Hammer, tussle over the possession of a peach, an object that Oliver ultimately wins and withholds from Elio, in what might be read as a summation of their relationship, and one that also struggles to withstand the pressures of circumstance. The peach also signifies *that which is forbidden*: being an object of desire that torments the younger Elio, and Oliver's possession of it, an indication of his ultimate control. Where the peach differs from Kechiche's spaghetti, however, is in its immediate identity as a symbol of the flesh, and so explicitly erotic as to make a tired cliché of the scene. Adele's eating of spaghetti, by contrast, disgusts us as much as it might turn us on. The winding of wet noodles around the end of a fork is a performance that is usually only acquired in young adulthood – a rite of passage, in a way, that one must go through in order to enter a world of grown-up interactions, including dates, dinner parties and other such social events. But it is also one that is liable to leave us besmirched by the traces of its occurrence, red splatters of sauce that risk spoiling the clean slate of a shirt or a tablecloth. Spaghetti, depending on the vantage point and setting, might be variously considered an emblem of refinement, or unruliness. It is both the provision of high-end restaurants, but also casual, thrown-together after-school dinners. It is an unstable symbol, and one that we attribute different meanings to depending on context and circumstance.

The same of course might be said of Adele's character, who on the one hand appears worldly, defiant and sexual outside of the family home, but vulnerable, small and childlike within it. This summarises the experience of early womanhood in general quite accurately, I believe, and a time when many are tasked with pulling away from the home and its patriarchal expectations of innocence and maidenly good virtue, while simultaneously testing the bounds of safety in a world that is prone to objectify and exploit. As Adele's character proves, this process of severance and maturity is one of trial and error, of wild lurches into the unknown, and timid retreats back into the family fold: an experience that is achieved by increments and many false starts.

Discussion of Adele's age and relative inexperience and, by extension, the actor Exarchopoulos's, naturally leads us to a conversation about the film's controversy, and specifically the accusation of its porny male gaze. I tend to agree with Manohla Dargis of the *New York Times* that there is truth in this, not to mention an over-emphasising of the duality between innocence and sexuality, in a way that often compounds stereotypes of a male fantasy: the idea that the naive and clueless Adele is exposed to a world of sensuality and pleasure by her more sexually experienced partner.[3] There is no harm in the filming of sex scenes, for which Exarchopoulos offered her full consent. But their handling by the male director jars with the rest of the film, and a story that is elsewhere charged with expectation and promise – something that is created by the film's extraordinarily slow pace and frustrating attention to detail. Rather than continuing this atmosphere, the sex scenes seem to place it on hold to facilitate a flat spectacle. The stilted conversations and moments of boredom, but also laughter and elation, do not feature in these scenes that are focused instead on arousing the viewer. In turn, the two women are reduced to performers in the non-acting sense, their story suspended for our voyeuristic pleasure. Nevertheless, I also agree with the committee at the 2013 Cannes Film Festival (including Ang Lee, Steven Spielberg and Nicole Kidman) who awarded it the Palme d'Or, that the film is an otherwise astute and sympathetic portrayal of romantic attachment, an achievement that is overwhelmingly as a result of the two central performances.

On account of that slow pace and attention to detail, however, both Exarchopoulos and Seydoux's performances are afforded the luxury of being both slight and naturalistic outside of the aforementioned sex scenes. With an accuracy that can be startling for those who have experienced anything similar, Exarchopoulos's Adele conveys the vulnerabilities of youth and inexperience, but also feeling out of one's depth among people of a higher social standing. At the film's start she is a schoolgirl and oblivious to certain qualities of refinement, favouring a style of dress that is oversized and slouchy, and with hair that is loosely fixed in a casual ponytail. The portrayal is obvious but perhaps not inaccurate, of a state-school teenage girl. At home, and in the first of the film's spaghetti scenes, she eats dinner with her parents over the table but in front of the TV. Here the dish is presented in a large vat for the three family members to serve themselves. Praise is effusive and all-round, as Adele and her father both thank Adele's mother for what she has made, and Adele readily consumes her first plate and then goes back for seconds, letting the sauce spill across her lips and cheeks and occasionally licking her knife to ensure that no morsel is missed. Much more likely than a comment about Adele's voracious sexual appetite is an idea of innocent abundance. There is a point about body image, and the ability to freely enjoy food in the years prior to considering oneself a sexual object and participant in capitalism.

This early dinner scene provides a portrait of a mother who is busy and a daughter who identifies food with a sense of pleasure, above formality or ritual. There is a practicality to the family's interactions, with conversations being solely focused on the matter of eating and the majority of each person's attention otherwise directed towards the TV, as if the main drive is to be freed from the responsibility of having to talk. So much conservative expectation is placed on the family dinner setting and its site of 'connection' and conversation, but when 'putting on a face' is such a burden of many lower-paid jobs, particularly those in the service and hospitality sectors, for example, that expectation in the current economic reality, can be tyrannical, even cruel. (Incidentally, the need to be jovial and conversational at work was the original definition of 'emotional labour', first coined by sociologist Arlie Russell Hochschild; a term that has since then been reimagined to mean any act of kindness or generosity towards another person).[4]

There is a beauty in this scene, and it derives from the lack of judgement that is evident between the members of the family. The ease with which they enjoy their meal, without needing to talk and without even flinching at the sound of loud bites being made – even a burp from Adele! – is one that can elude many of us in the years after leaving the family fold. To say that the communication is non-existent would also be derogatory and untrue, as in the place of verbal interaction exists a language of silent cues and gestures that are no less comforting and indicative of love: glances that convey appreciation, plates being handed to each other in a gesture for second servings. The relaxed familiarity of the scene also demonstrates a reverence for the food itself, and the pleasure of sustenance. By reverse, we can read a demotion of food, and that same enjoyment, in forms of dining that dogmatically insist on the presence of conversation and formality. The class commentary is slight but important here then, quietly showcasing the loveliness in a style of eating that has been mocked and frequently blamed for a variety of social ills.

A few scenes later, the family are once again gathered to share a meal of spaghetti, only this time they are joined by Adele's lover Emma, played by Seydoux. At that point Adele's parents still believe that Emma is their daughter's mentor and tutor, creating a dramatic irony and tension as several misunderstandings unfold. Any reading of this scene however, must account for the very specific ways in which class dynamics play out in French culture specifically, where communal dining around shared pots of hearty food is still associated with lower-middle and working-class life (where this has long ceased to be a feature of working-class life in Britain and other cultures more indebted to an American cuisine whose emphasis is on prefabricated convenience and ease). By the film's logic and based on personal experience as well, in French culture there seems to still exist a traditional delineation between middle-class refinement, and working-class communal fare: working families, for reasons of food being cheaper and more freely available due to lower reliance on imports, not to mention the protections on worker's rights and hours that are still marginally better than in the UK, large home-cooked meals are still somewhat more accessible to working people than they are here. It is also crucial to acknowledge that Adele is by no means poor, in a dimension of the film that lends it a unique fascination, highlighting as it does the importance that is nevertheless placed on the slightest differences in taste, mannerism and cultural sensibility that exist between people of only slightly divergent social and economic standing – the *narcissism of small differences*, described previously, and how this plays out in the creation of so much shame, humiliation and crises of identity.

We can easily deduce, however, that by Adele's mother's choice of spaghetti, the family is being marked as lower-middle class and certainly at a social disadvantage to their new guest, who eats in a quieter and more restrained way than Adele, always with a closed mouth and never licking her knife or letting food gather at the corners of her mouth, but delicately sucking on a single strand of pasta in turn. If we were led to believe that such reticence was simply an expression of politeness and discomfort in being an outsider, perhaps indicative of an uncertainty as to whether the parents know that she is romantically involved with their daughter, then this is quashed only a few moments later when Emma says, perhaps with a degree of passive aggression, *bon appétit*, after the other family members have already started eating. Whether other viewers share my reading of this event or not, what is much less debatable is the fact of Emma's confidence in being able to convey to her hosts a personal set of behaviours and preferences. She does not eat of her own volition, but must be invited by Adele's father, whose manner is curt. This might be for reasons of offence at Emma's reticence, but also a general distrust for the progressive values embodied by her vivid blue hair (which Adele's mother describes as 'artistic', to which Emma only offers a mild 'thank you' in response).

Emma is visibly disappointed when it becomes clear Adele has not yet told her parents about their relationship, and when Adele's mother thanks Emma for schooling her daughter in philosophy, Emma struggles to maintain conversation while seeking to avoid opening her mouth while eating, something that Adele flagrantly ignores. In all these small quirks is a comment on the contending upsets that occur in the process of coming out to one's family, and the unfair deceit that queer people are often forced to maintain in order to satisfy the prejudices of a society that they are nevertheless required to appeal to in various ways and in order to maintain peaceful relationships. A degree of sadness and discomfort must be accounted for, then, but Emma's behaviour also seems to suggest an unrelated disdain towards the lifestyle of her hosts.

As an artist, Emma presents as something of an anomaly to a family who possess a pedestrian concern for their daughter's financial prosperity. It is an understandable concern, even if it is not universally shared. Such pragmatism seems to elude Emma, who despite the gentleness with which it is conveyed, seems affronted by their concern for her life choices. As if instructing both girls, Adele's father reminds them that it is difficult for an artist to make any money and to sustain themselves. 'It is important to have an artistic side,' he says, 'but you need a real job too. To earn a living.' Almost as if he is reassuring himself of her straightness, this is followed by Adele's father then making enquiries about Emma's boyfriend, to which Emma replies that he works in finance and is therefore able to support her – something that assuages both parents' concerns, and even causes Adele's mother to let out a small *whoop*.

The scene is one that many can relate to, encapsulating so much that is relevant to generational differences in attitude towards sexuality, but also labour and money. It shows plainly how the opening up of higher education meant an opening up of the suburban domestic sphere to a wider variety of opinions and ideas. The overwhelmingly positive effects of which must also be factored alongside the many fresh tensions that it created, too, whose documentation will never be complete and remains a preoccupation of my work. In this scene we witness the implications of cultural capital; of Emma, student at the Beaux Arts, bristling against the prejudicial, mercenary concerns of her petit bourgeois hosts, whose concern for money reads as a lack of imagination and a stifling of possibility. High cultural capital, born of a university degree and exposure to certain cultural strains and ideas, creates the sense that one has recourse to their wits or creativity in the market economy, something that can seem too flimsy and uncertain to older generations. Nevertheless, Emma is a guest, and the derision, though slight and testament to Seydoux's virtuosic performance, is detectable. While Adele's parents hold beliefs that are outdated, and in many ways hostile to free expression and queerness specifically, and their tone of quiet superiority and authority doubtless galling to their guest, they are nevertheless inquisitive, warm and genuinely curious. Rather than addressing the issue at hand, which would be impossible, Emma lets her discomfort and disapproval be known through a scornful comment on something completely unrelated – the food.

'The pasta is delicious,' she says. 'Simple but ... very good.'

The dark side of *plain, simple*, then, requires a qualifier in order to be transformed into a compliment. 'Simple' – the word used in French and favoured in the English translation – carries a wide array of meanings, including both the unrefined and the uncouth, not to mention the plainly stupid. Whatever prejudices Emma feels towards Adele's family predate their discussion about art and sexuality. While we sympathise with Emma in having to navigate this situation, which is best described as being ambiently patriarchal, and not overtly homophobic, it does not justify Emma's derision towards the expressions of their class. And yet it is clear from her statement, and the smugness with which she gently mocks the family thereafter (by upholding such a far-fetched untruth that she is married to a banker), that Emma feels vindicated in her judgements.

Despite its tensions and its anguishes, for all of these reasons, this scene remains one of my favourite in cinema, capturing the tension that has defined the past few decades in terms socioeconomic shifts and electoral outcomes, particularly on account of how oblivious both parties remain to their own bigotries – the parents' failure to look beyond their own, committed world view that women should marry financially viable men and pursue lucrative careers, and the resulting sense of justification that Emma feels with respect to her own prejudices of class and manners. It also highlights the fact that food, whose role in our lives is so fundamental, and so emotive as a result, often forms one of the most fraught and complex sites of interplay between the generations and the classes. Behind a vocabulary of good health, quality connection and the supposedly therapeutic effects of cooking, lies a well of anger, confusion, longing and pride.

In a later scene, Adele creates the same dish for a party to celebrate Emma's graduation, in an event that also serves the purpose of allowing Emma to network with other graduates and people from the local art scene. By this point Adele has found a job as a schoolteacher, but on the evening in question she is out of place, emphasised by her being alone at the beginning of the scene, preparing dumplings as well as spaghetti in a kitchen where she receives no help. Without any objection from her co-hosts and guests, Adele assumes the role of caterer, one that seems to bring her comfort and distraction from the people who otherwise show her little interest.

In a speech that is given later to her peers, Emma acknowledges Adele as her muse. The description makes Adele uncomfortable, as it would many of us, and we see in the resulting expression the same dislocation that had fallen over her features at her parent's dinner table a few scenes earlier. 'She also cooked all of the food,' Emma adds, and the cheers prompted by this compliment do much more to correct the awkwardness of the last, prompting Adele to smile, and perhaps momentarily, even bask in the glow of their praise.

The guests continue to talk among themselves while all but one person fails to consider whether Adele has enough food to serve herself. The guests are demanding, requesting additional sauce and parmesan, and afterwards paying little regard to the effort that has been made as the more important matter of art world debate takes hold. Emma's involvement in that world ultimately contributes to the demise of the relationship – a fact that is neatly summarised by the film's final scene in which Adele's attendance at a gallery opening for Emma's work held years later. Adele spends much of the time wandering around aimlessly and by herself, while fellow guests discuss the scene. Meanwhile proceedings are accompanied by delicate canapés, served on large platters and which guests are invited to help themselves to, delicately lifting each morsel between their forefinger and thumb and munching on them between sentences. If the food symbolism was ambiguous before, then the stark contrast between the spaghetti and the finger-food would make the class commentary apparent, in addition to where the film's sympathies ultimately lie.

Adele realises that moderation will be necessary in order to assimilate, and, on account of how little respect is extended towards her both on the occasion of the speech and at the exhibition opening, finally develops the self-respect and determination to leave, walking down the street alone and towards what we hope will be a future of much more empathy, curiosity and pride in the life choices she has made. All of which can be felt while still acknowledging the good done by the formative experience that she has nevertheless gained in the years spent with Emma, and without pouring scorn on Emma who pursued a love that society had censured.

Reflecting on this film always brings up uncomfortable memories of passing flings and fleeting crushes entering my parents' home and, forming part of what I believed to be an obligatory transition into a person of respectable taste and high social standing, allowing them to pass all kinds of judgements and make condescending remarks. Not only this, but there were moments too when no such external voice or interloper was even required, and it was me who poured scorn on the habits and preferences that I had previously enjoyed and participated in without question, imposing my new tastes as though they were fact. Where house guests and the precocious teenager that I was might have withheld passing judgement on interior design choices or personal decisions related to fashion or beauty – believing, rightly, that this would constitute bad manners – food always seemed to be fair game. What was often little more than insecurity and internalised shame towards my own class status and body image concerns, was instead framed as an unassailable truth and concern for the wellbeing of myself and others.

Food sanctimony

When thinking about food and taste, it can be difficult, if not impossible, to separate concern for health from the wider cultural setting in which much of the health discussion exists. One foodstuff, which has almost become an emblem of intergenerational conflict, is coffee. Elders are generally tolerant of a powdered form while younger people prefer it ground: the two types that are usually referred to are 'real' or 'instant'. Instant coffee, for clarity, is created by dehydrating previously brewed coffee through a process known as freeze drying or spray drying, such that it can be rehydrated through the addition of water, in a process that is far more amenable to busy schedules and situations where the preparation of caffeinated drinks needs to be carried out in haste. No consensus exists on whether instant or ground coffee is better for health, only that the former usually contains much less caffeine. As an aside, but worth mentioning, the main complaint made against instant coffee is to do with taste, something that would seem to be much less subjective than questions of aesthetic judgement discussed elsewhere in this book, but which in reality is much the same. What interests me are definitions, however. The process by which instant coffee is created constitutes only one or two additional steps in a process that otherwise involves plucking, drying, transporting over thousands of miles, roasting and grinding. Pedantic as it is to point this out, the summoning of authenticity seems to be more about a belief in antiquated methods of preparation – of believing that brewing somehow constitutes something more real than rehydration. There are echoes here of the more naturalistic emphasis on beauty, with its insistence on a twelve-step skincare routine as opposed to a topical beauty fix through makeup; but also, the homespun clothing styles and home fixes that have been popularised and pitted against quicker, more mechanised solutions. Often sanctimony towards certain food items that would seem to be connected with nutritional value bear no such concern.

The matter-of-fact way in which certain foodstuffs are nevertheless announced as being superior to others often also overlooks speed as a measure of value. Despite knowing that working people are time-poor with limited capacity to indulge in drawn-out processes of so-called self-care, and that this only becomes worse the further one travels down the pay scale, where multiple jobs are a necessity of survival, rarely does this extend to an understanding of what might be driving differences of consumer choice. Nor do we seem prepared to admit that what we value for supposedly humble reasons of an artisanal preference, is in fact tied up in the tacit conveyance of abundant time and therefore wealth. This becomes tangled in a harmful language of moral absolutes and judgements. When magazine editorials and social media users stress the affordability of certain, supposedly more healthy food items than others, in a bid, supposedly, to encourage more working people to eat well, they are often wilfully overlooking the way that wealth operates in today's society. For many it is not a limitation in being able to afford the fresh, organic ground coffee, or other groceries with which to make a fresh meal, but the free time, energy and self-esteem with which to engage in its methods of preparation.

What's more, to really challenge prejudices of class in food culture would require the disassociation of nutritional value from morality. What if the ultimate aspiration, health-wise, was to eliminate all forms of stress? Who can possibly measure the benefits to health of food preparation being streamlined and sped up – the reduction of stress that results from this, and how this compares to the impact of whatever synthetic additives might have been included? But even beyond this, who is to say that health is the ultimate aim at all? Matters that should be the purview of each person and their doctor have an uncomfortable way of becoming the subject of unsolicited advice from online health bloggers, influencers and diet brands. What if the ultimate aspiration, food-wise, was not to extend one's life and achieve optimal fitness, but instead, to proffer as much enjoyment as possible during the few short years that we are alive? Why does the serotonin released from drinking a sugary strawberry milkshake not factor into an assessment of health and wellbeing, and who can really say if the positive effect is still weighed in favour of the vitamins imparted by the organic smoothie alternative? What if values associated with food existed outside of tightly held belief systems and formed part of an experience that we might have never previously considered?

Quite often, what is really a question of aesthetics and a sanctimony rooted in Christian conservative values passes under a supposed concern for wellbeing, as the preference for natural produce and home-cooked food is presented as a moral duty to one's body, one's family and one's National Health Service, which must not be subject to undue strain as a result of people's careless lifestyles. This concern rarely stretches to other, equally harmful health issues born of malnutrition, for example, not to mention the litany of so-called vices approved by affluent demographics more often than not responsible for dictating everybody else's consumption habits – among them regular wine drinking, regular flying, late nights, but also, regular use of cocaine and the recreational use of Ritalin. The reason these health concerns rarely attract attention is because they either do not make themselves physically apparent, or if they do, these appearances also do not challenge the fearful, puritanical gaze of a society that is increasingly preoccupied with notions of self-restraint and effacement.

In so many articles, varying in their motivations from the patronising if well-meaning, to the downright derogatory – explaining the ways in which a working-class mother (and it is always a mother) might feed her family, with shopping lists of organic items from the vegetable aisle – there is a clear denial of the need for pleasure, satisfaction, enjoyment and fun. A food culture that constantly emphasises the benefits of delayed gratification neglects to recognise that systemic inequality means gratification for many people is always delayed and never given – that for the vast majority of people, endurance is never offset by periods of total indulgence and that for most, languorous food production methods in the week will never be abated by a Friday night visit to a fancy restaurant or several lavish holidays a year. Instead, most people are forced, under current economic conditions, to grab their moments of pleasure where they can, and cheaply.

In recent years there has emerged a trend on social media of users smugly recounting the affordable meals they have costed up and which disprove the complaints of hardship being made by poorer people everywhere: the sort of tweet that reads, 'I made my son a cheese omelette for 25p', 'In my day we ate sugar sandwiches and were happy with it', and, 'a pound of liver costs less than a McDonald's – tell me why you can't live off that?' What these facile assessments fail to account for – in fact, what they attempt to deny and censure – is the basic human need for, and right to, pleasure, and how the threshold for achieving pleasure is adjusted to GDP and is always, by definition, relativistic. Just as a child of the 1930s might have been afflicted by shame if forced to eat a diet of Victorian gruel, so a child forced to eat cheese omelettes and cooked liver every night, while their peers enjoy the pleasures of a lavish meal, would suffer in much the same way. And yet many middle-class people, labouring under a false sense of their own moral virtue, go online to broadcast this heinous attitude day after day.

We find in this tendency an echo of what Bourdieu was referring to as well when discussing the French lifestyle magazine *Connaissance de la Campagne*, of the preference for handed-down recipes and 'real' home-cooked food by people for whom tradition had not been made a dirty word. 'A pot of "home-made gherkins", "made to Grandma's recipe" and brought to the table with the appropriate verbal accompaniment,' writes Bourdieu, 'as when exhibiting the "little picture by an eighteenth-century French master" spotted at the antique dealer's, or the "exquisite little piece of furniture" unearthed in a junk shop – symbolizes [sic.] the squandering of time and a competence which can only be acquired by long frequentation of old, cultivated people and things, that is, membership of an ancient group, the sole guarantee of possession of all the properties which are endowed with the highest distinctive value because they can only be accumulated over time.'

Patron saints of sustenance

One wishes the British chef Jamie Oliver had been shown this quotation. Having made his name in *The Naked Chef* (1999–2001), a prime-time TV cookery show in which he was tasked with rustling up delicious 'grub' all while wearing a windbreaker and contending with situations afflicting the modern man, supposedly – cooking for his girlfriend after a night out clubbing or having to please his indie music band, Scarlett Division – Oliver expanded his ambitions in the mid-2000s to embark on a campaign that would install healthy eating habits in the homes of the British public. This effort would include the creation of *Jamie's Ministry of Food* in 2008, an initiative comprising a TV show, cookbook and cookery course, whose name was taken from the wartime institution dedicated to managing Britain's rations. Filmed in Rotherham, one of the country's poorest areas, the show's producers, and Oliver, heaped scorn, albeit unintentionally, onto an already maligned community.

'As more and more families eat more and more junk,' declares the commentary on the first episode, played over a toddler chewing on an unidentifiable object and people opening the polystyrene casing of a takeaway meal, 'Britain is on the verge of a health disaster.' The focus then shifts to footage of Oliver driving along the motorway, while the voiceover explains that he is on a mission to fix the problem by getting 'an entire British town to teach each other to cook'.

The intentions are good, and by comparison to the vitriol that had been directed towards the diets of people on low incomes elsewhere in the tabloid press, Oliver's efforts are generous, even sympathetic (in the episode, Oliver meets one woman who had been dubbed a 'fast food mum' by the press, and offers her a platform on which to speak). The aim of transforming food culture for the better and improving health standards for people everywhere, had its merits. The insensitivity was caused by a failure to properly address the economic conditions that had led to the popularisation of so-called fast-food, and particularly the scarcity of time among people having to raise families in harsh conditions, work multiple jobs, or indeed both.

Oliver was by no means the creator of this tendency in TV broadcasting of the 2000s and 2010s, in which working people were often sent up and humiliated for their life choices and behaviours – and he was certainly not its worst culprit. He did not resemble those TV presenters who had affected a ghoulish persona to boost TV viewing figures, after a style first popularised by the TV talent show judge Simon Cowell. But these characters were also outsized and farcical. Oliver, by contrast, positioned himself as a man of the people, pioneering a style of media output that was no less condemnatory, but much more polite. Oliver did not lecture his subjects, but coaxed them gently. He seemed to be genuinely invested in improving people's standards of living and allowing them to live more healthily. Only as the author and critic Owen Hatherley has pointed out, those efforts 'foundered on the disinclination of any plausible British government to antagonise the supermarkets and sundry manufacturers who funnel money to the two main political parties'.[5]

Oliver has since spoken about feeling intimidated by food industry bosses, during his attempts to lobby the government and improve food standards for the British public.[6] Met with the resistance of policy makers, and the vested interest of those who wielded the most power over Britain's food supply, his efforts suffered from the fact that they appeared to be targeting only single mothers and dinner ladies on TV.

As a result, the healthy food movement led by Oliver would be somewhat confined to the domain of publicity and media – the realm of the spectacle. His popularity created a new style of well-meaning and benevolent home cooking show and book, whose emphasis was as much on 'helping' us as relaying delicious recipes. The result of this is that the burden of responsibility for tackling the nation's health issues would lie solely at the door of the consumer. Nutrition, diet and health would be falsely reduced to a question of *good* versus *bad* taste. Oliver's shows would find a home among similar styles of TV programming in which affluent presenters lectured members of the public on their poor life choices and rotten homes. In all of the well-meaning propaganda about the pleasure that could be found in the preparation of real food, was a failure to recognise that culinary creation of any kind is the least priority of people living in the demoralising conditions of many post-industrial towns. Noble efforts to present meals that only required a few ingredients also failed to account for the mental tax involved in ensuring that those ingredients were bought, and the added burden of having to shop every day, or else develop elaborate meal plans at the beginning of the working week. In an age where most people were not wandering back from work or school via a high street (these had all but been destroyed), but forced to drive by car to enormous, out of town supermarkets, the idea of shopping joyfully and within one's means, also seemed increasingly far-fetched. As a result, the emphasis on how 'quick' and 'easy' these recipes might be, placed an even larger degree of shame on those prevented by circumstance from producing such meals. If there was a health crisis in the UK, then its cause was not the habits or tastes of individual families, but the working conditions that prevented people from having the agency and freedom to prioritise their health. It was a result of a society that had been given over entirely to corporate greed, and the devaluation of human life as a result. In such a climate, the repeat spectacle of a person seeking to rev us all up into a fresh-food revolution was not only facile, but rightly stood accused of superficiality when little was being done to also tackle the real causes at play.

Arguably just as egregious as all of this was the leveraging of the family in adjacent marketing campaigns. Books by

Oliver that carried titles such as *Superfood: Family Classics* (2016) and *Together: Memorable Meals Made Easy* (2021) – to say nothing of their generic sentiment and clear ambition to expand the repertoire of sellable items under the Jamie Oliver brand name – carried a message of sanctimony and condescension with respect to the nuclear family and the conservative belief in the necessity of a nightly meal around the dinner table. While posing no objection to this idea itself, its insistence as part of a model of respectability is one laden with assumptions of class and wealth, not least among which is the belief that people everywhere have the means and room for a family-sized dining table. But beyond this, too, a subtle but profound stereotype was being reinforced, which seemed to form a part of a wider tendency towards nostalgia, of the healthy person also being the one who conformed most thoroughly to the social expectations of the conservative ideal with its emphasis on heterosexual fidelity, child rearing and maternal hosting.

This carried into the output of influencers whose advice had nothing to do with dieting, but everything to do with a sort of nebulous definition of wholesomeness desirable for reasons having to do with pastel-coloured Smeg fridges and Agas. Quietly, a connection was being made between slimness, wealth and certain traditional expectations about family, domestic labour and gender. Cookery shows and books had gone from explicating culinary processes that might have otherwise only been available to the trained specialist, to being far more about *what* we ate, and instructive on the matter of our diets and our lifestyles. The 'clean' food movement would extend to the idea of clean lives and clean people, while also insinuating the existence of its opposite, as health claims and moral virtues started to converge.[7] What was ostensibly billed as a more relatable, less condemnatory diet culture than the more aggressively corporate styles of the past, transformed something that was at least confined to one, very limited aspect of our eating habits, into something far more universal and profound. These guides seemed to imply that it wasn't an adjustment of one or two decisions per day that was needed – the swapping out of one foodstuff for another – but a wholesale transformation of our very existence and moral outlook, to align more closely with the habits that these influencers exhibited.

All of which forms part of a wider cultural tendency towards totems of a fetishised and fictional austerity, similar to the kind discussed in previous chapters. It is here that we find ourselves returning to the nineteenth-century film set that now exists in bourgeois enclaves on the edges of major cities, where between the smoked glass filament lamps and sooty walls are craftspeople in overalls peddling baked goods and edible exotica from far-off lands. This is what Owen Hatherley has dubbed 'austerity consumerism'. If people had survived rationing proudly on account of necessity during the world wars, then consumers in the 2010s would be sold a synthetic version of this. Perhaps it caught on by assuaging the feeling of hopelessness and despair caused by the financial hardship that was a result of something so pathetic and avoidable as the greed of incompetent bankers and the failure of the state to properly intervene – creating a Blitz Spirit from our rage.

The trend that emerged at that time, for overpriced

groceries arranged in a style that might have been adopted by a gourd seller on market day in nineteenth-century France, has shown little indication that it will ever go away. Stores that adopted this nostalgia often carry awnings and silver metal bowls, along with mason jars of assorted grains for dispensing into brown bags. Their creation coincided with several food-related festivals catering to an older demographic, compelled by the idea of reliving its youth but without the will or constitution for all-night parties – events including the excruciatingly titled Big Feastival hosted on the land of former Blur guitarist Alex James and co-hosted with Oliver. From their jolly branding to the spokespeople who would be quoted endlessly on the subject of quality food and wanting more people to 'eat better', nothing could have been practically further from the truth, as these events, much like the preference for items of modernist design in fashion and interiors, were overpriced and committed to selling us more and more products of an aestheticised wholesomeness.

What might be casually dismissed as a bit of good fun creates the conditions for a vapid, ahistorical approach to tackling the country's food crisis, making systemic failures a matter of taste and preference. At the same time, the language of inclusivity peddled by these events and their wider culture only serves to further stigmatise working people by making a lack of participation seem like a poor choice of lifestyle. By insisting that healthy food could be jolly, speedy and affordable, anyone who now failed to replicate the same effect for themselves would carry the blame for whatever ills – be those physical, behavioural or spiritual – that now befell them and their children. All of which conspired with messaging that was often coming from central government, about the necessity of taking personal accountability for the causes of obesity – a condition whose associated health complaints, to stress again, are brought about just as readily by other conditions, including malnutrition, smoking, excess drinking and of course, stress. The latter of which is only exacerbated by the coterie of smug TV influencers smiling out at us from every cookery book, phone and TV screen, with their poorly informed judgements and deranged glee.

Holy bread

As a symbol of life and security – something so foundational to wellbeing it is synonymous with god himself in some religions – bread can help us understand just how prevalent and petty are many of these consumer anxieties. When bread became unaffordable to the working classes of Paris at the end of the eighteenth century, it prompted thousands of people, mainly women, to organise and march on Versailles, in an event that is broadly considered to have started the French Revolution.

Today bread is big business and extremely fashionable, predominantly in the sourdough form that has gone from being the purview of elite bakeries, to being found on the more expensive shelves of mainstream supermarkets. The superior health claim does hold some degree of truth here: sourdough bread generally scores lower on the glycemic index than bread that is made from synthetic forms of yeast, meaning that the body processes its sugar content more gradually and therefore with less likelihood of causing harmful spikes in blood-sugar levels. But the difference is slight, and beyond this, and depending on the type of wheat used, of course, both sourdough and more commercial forms of bread are broadly equivalent in terms of their nutritional value. Despite this, and as the journalist Dan Hancox has pointed out, the price of a loaf in London can vary from as little as 36p from a supermarket, to as much as £5 in a nearby bakery.[8] This is driven by what behavioural economists refer to as marginal utility – the secondary sense of luxury and indulgence that attends an object – rather than total utility – that is, its basic necessity and role in everyday life. This distorts basic supply-and-demand models, coaxing us towards consumer choices that are based on wants that are liable to be manipulated by advertisers, trends and social pressure.

Its relative health benefits aside, aesthetic concerns are also driving the sourdough boom. Forming part of a wider, nostalgic turn in consumer desire, it also represents a shift away from the faceless machinery of the modern food industry, and into the hands of dedicated craftspeople. Support for this shift is not remotely misplaced, and the independent model of food production supports workers and the environment far more effectively than any mass-production model ever could. But when that assessment is transposed into a value judgement of the object itself, and the people who consume it, those responsible are prone to fuel a culture war in which our tastes are wilfully misread as barometers of identity, political persuasion and moral purity.

Again, it is a failure to recognise the myriad, competing requirements that dictate any consumer decision – if it can even be called that – which might not be apparent from appearances or without an intimate understanding of the lives and experiences of those involved, that leads to the sanctimony with which the sourdough craze is discussed. This is only emphasised by its place within a visual universe that prioritises a bygone age, glossed of its bigotries of racism, sexism, homophobia and consumption, and instead posited as some kind of idyll, composed solely of overalls and burly bakers whose faces are smeared with flour, burlap bags tied with string, and jolly maidens unburdened by the considerations of work and childcare. Nostalgia is also hard-baked (!) into the sourdough mythos. This is not just because it predates the more modern methods of bread making, but because the 'starter' on which it depends – a pre-ferment mixture composed of flour and water that contains a colony of microorganisms, including yeast and lactic acid bacteria, that allow the bread to rise – has the potential to be many centuries old. These cultures, which are alive (if not, presumably, sentient) are often afforded pet-like status, and cared for and maintained by their bakery with a sense of love and duty. After all, they are unique, and owing to their interaction with the external environment, also susceptible to changing character depending on location. One sourdough starter will produce bread of a very different taste and texture to another. As such, it is not uncommon for starters to be passed down through the generations, and for many bakeries to claim that theirs was first created in the distant past. To purchase a loaf of sourdough, to slice it and to toast it and to eat it with a little piece of cheese on top, is – as the lore confected by many bakeries would have us believe – to be a part of history itself. With so many recurring and worsening crises of capitalism, and the threat of ecological collapse, the often rose-tinted view with which we look upon the past is automatically extended to these objects of a bygone craftsmanship, stacked in heaps in the windows of today's luxury baking establishments. The white, square, squishy loaves found wrapped in plastic in the supermarket just down the road, carrying the weight of responsibility for the whole of modernity and the Frankenstein food industry created by it.

Resurrecting artisanal and antiquated methods of food preparation is to food culture what natural skin has been to beauty, homespun threads have been to fashion and teak modernism has been to interior design – and in every case, if sustainability was an objective then this was secondary to style. All form part of a preference for a 'simpler' time, where 'organic' and 'homemade' are equivalent to the 'simple' or the 'natural' – a phenomenon which, as it evolved, started to encroach on the language of survivalism. During the COVID-19 pandemic, the sanctimony surrounding food, found fertile ground among a population that was anxious and static, who became preoccupied by the idea of being able to create basic foodstuffs like bread, yoghurt, pickles and stews for fear that supply routes would be permanently affected. The idea of endless free time was circulated, as each new post made a 'we' of the people who were not required to leave the house and attend their jobs, or else become a full-time carer to their loved ones. The mass scare of a bread shortage briefly gripped the British public, causing a spike in bread-making and of people sharing the use of their sourdough starter kits online.

In this, I was reminded of what Doris Lessing wrote about in *The Memoirs of a Survivor,* her chilling 1974 fictional account of life in London following a nameless apocalyptic event. 'When nothing, or very little, was left of what we had been used to, had taken for granted even ten years before, we went on talking and behaving as if those old forms were still ours. And indeed, order of the old kind – food, amenities, even luxuries, *did* exist at higher levels, we all knew that; though of course those who enjoyed these things did not draw attention to themselves. Order could also exist in pockets, of space, of time – through periods of weeks and months or in a particular district. Inside them, people would live and talk and even think as if nothing had changed. When something really bad happened, as when an area got devastated, people might move out for days, or weeks, to stay with relatives or friends, and then move back, perhaps to a looted house, to take up their job, their housekeeping – their order. We can get used to anything at all; this is a commonplace, of course, but perhaps you have to live through such a time to see how horribly true it is. There is nothing that people won't try to accommodate into "ordinary life".'[9]

I became convinced that a global pandemic and the immediate threat of global warming had created a tendency to gamify despair – to aestheticise the imperatives of survival and absorb them into a language of tepid and condescending lifestyle advice, overlaid with a nostalgic filter. I also became worried about the opportunities this created for people to seize on that repressed despair and promote other facets of a bygone existence, that tended towards the more culturally conservative, in terms of reaffirming harmful ideas about gender, beauty and people's place in society. The sense of relish for the opportunity to revive a wartime spirit frightened me, particularly in its reimagining of a hardship whose traumas were real and long-lasting, into a badge of honour and a perverse aspiration. A harmful asceticism in food culture, one that masked many dangerous prejudices about weight and class, collided with a fetishisation of austerity, transforming the happy act of eating into a challenge and an act of will.

Chapter Six

Leisure

You Can't Take It With You

UNKNOWN

A few years ago my friend Margaux and I took a holiday to Marseilles in the South of France. We settled on the location for its speed and affordability; Margaux is French and was living in Paris at the time, and I was living in London, so in each case, and according to Margaux's meticulous planning, it would only take a short train ride or flight. Ease of transit in getting there would be the least of our problems, it turned out, but we weren't to know that until a few hours after our arrival. Margaux, for the record, is often organising trips and activities for her friends, being as she is one the kindest, most organised and generous people I have ever met. I am quite different. There was the time, for example, when Margaux registered us for the Paris Half Marathon, an event for which I travelled to France but ultimately ended up making both of us watch from a nearby café over Bloody Marys, themselves a cure for the hangover that was also my fault. I am not proud of this admission, and suspect at times and to an outsider at least, our friendship has looked like one of conscientious enthusiasm versus a chaotic apathy. But this is not how I experience it. I love Margaux in ways I have loved few other people in my life, and envy her ability to see far enough past the end of her own nose to orchestrate some of the most beautiful and brilliant moments in the lives of the people who know her.

I had little reason to believe that our first morning in Marseilles would be any different. Arriving to meet Margaux at the main station from where we hailed a cab that took us on towards the port, Margaux explained that we would be taking a sailboat to the Calanques, a series of inlets off the coast of Marseilles famed for their still waters and abundant wildlife. Marvelling at her logistical prowess as I always did, and to which she would normally offer some self-effacing remark about it being nothing, on this occasion and for the first time at least she was much more insistent, a look of genuine amazement in place of the false modesty as she explained to me that it had all been handled through a tool connected to the house-sharing website Airbnb. The Airbnb Experiences feature allows tourists to book activities with local people, offering the chance for cooking classes, walking tours and wellness retreats. If I have one criticism – and it is only one – of my dear friend and great love Margaux, it is her total lack of cynicism towards this and anything like it, and the eyeroll with which she met my subsequent tirade about the expansion of the so-called 'experience economy' and its tendency to commodify everyday activities. I had read articles about how high streets had become overrun by escape rooms, novelty dining experiences and ball pits, lamenting the sell-off of public space and the upscaled, overpriced and 'immersive' dimensions of previously simple activities, like going to the cinema. The experience economy was a hot topic of newspapers and magazines at the time, as consumer trends had shifted to incorporate new levels of gimmickry in the ways that people spent their evenings and weekends; a phenomenon that had been partly attributed to the expansion of social media and the pressure felt by everyone to broadcast a kooky and interesting impression to the outside world.

This line of discussion was apparently not in the spirit of being on holiday, however, and so I learned to be quiet, as we pulled up to the port and as I helped Margaux carry the baguettes, boxes of wine and wheels of cheese that she had bought for the occasion. The image of us then reclining on the leather seats that lined the sailboat's deck, fixing our hair under our headscarves – the image of me, in particular, wearing large hoop earrings bought from a gold shop in Birmingham, and which would soon be involuntarily sacrificed to the seas – inspires pity. As does the memory of how fondly I looked upon our skipper, a friendly Welshman and recent ex-pat who kept saying how thankful he was to finally have people to share his new hobby with.

Friends of mine with more seafaring experience protest the level of horror with which I narrate the following events, insisting that we could not have been even half as close to death as we claimed. Still, whether or not our lives were at risk is not so important as the fact that it absolutely seemed as though they were, after we had left the port and been sailing for about half an hour, and as the city, with its remarkably dense urban structure, had faded to little more than a smudge on the horizon. At that point the waters went dark, mimicking that well-quoted refrain from Homer's *Odyssey*, 'the wine-dark sea', which had not occurred to me until that point as being a feature of the potential drowning experience for which I had paid £100. As the grey jelly of the sea threatened to swallow us whole, the wine that we had bought flew by the boxload in every direction, along with the baguettes and the wheels of cheese and the various other facets of a lifestyle we had been trying to emulate from Anthony Minghella's 1999 film adaptation of the Patricia Highsmith novel, *The Talented Mr Ripley*. All I have from the encounter, beyond vague memories of screaming curses to both Airbnb and the experience economy more generally, are two selfies taken from the safety of land when we finally docked at an island, after travelling further out to sea and a point at which the French coast was no longer visible (following the wisdom of our skipper that we needed to go with, rather than against, the winds). These photos, in which I possess the manic stare of a person who has just narrowly escaped death, and in which my hair constitutes a sort of mesmerising explosion on top of my head, now serve as proof to me of the absurdity in trying to become part of a group that was nowhere better satirised than in Highsmith's novels.[1]

The art of living

The leisure class, as mentioned previously, was a term coined by Thorstein Veblen to refer to a new economic group that had emerged at the end of the nineteenth century, along with the more advanced stages of industrial capitalism that had evolved in Western society. It was a group, previously undefined by such a subtly scathing moniker, that wore its wealth in frequent holidays and accomplishments in culture and sport. *The Talented Mr Ripley* holds a lens to the leisure class, particularly in the character of Dickie Greenleaf, played with a genius flair by the actor Jude Law in the film adaptation. Dickie is a man of no fixed abode or job, whose life instead is devoted to sunbathing in Italy and mastering the arts of jazz, martini-making and interior design. When Dickie's father tires of having to fund his son's lifestyle, he sends Tom Ripley to lure Dickie back to America. The story hinges on the reveal of Tom Ripley as a sociopath, skilled at playing both generations of the Greenleaf family to his own advantage, in what might be read as a revenge fantasy of the working class against those who have flagrantly embraced a life of minimal responsibility and economic concern. It is why the Ripley character remains so popular, despite his distinct lack of redeeming qualities, in what is a perfect riposte to the age-old adage, taught in creative writing classes and repeated constantly by the publishing industry, that characters need to be likeable in order for readers to be invested in them. Providing that the moral justifications chime with our own, it is actually quite surprising how much we will tolerate in our fictional characters with respect to violence and cruelty.

If Dickie is materialistic, then this is only a secondary motivation. He owns nice things, most of which seem to be inherited, but his primary concern is experience. In the same vein, he tends to also see people as serving his need for fun and hedonism, and as such, treats them cruelly and disposably. He has a university degree, but it is not clear why, or whether he has ever put his studies to good use. Tom Ripley, by contrast, starts out as a hotel porter and jobbing musician and puts an almost oppressive weight on matters of friendship and human connection, but also cultural understanding and education. Ripley is only able to deceive Dickie by convincing him that they had been friends at Princeton, a period of Dickie's life that he is already describing by his late twenties as a 'fog', and thereby disclosing the irrelevance of education to both his fortune and identity. Pierre Bourdieu observed in *Distinction* that people who relied on formal education for any degree of recognition or prosperity, continued to treat educational matters with a severity and seriousness throughout their lives, while more privileged individuals, exposed to these ideas ambiently and from an early age, did not.[2] This also explains why Ripley is a much more conscientious observer of good taste, where Dickie and his friends – particularly Freddie Miles, played to perfection by Philip Seymour Hoffman in the film adaptation – are far more carefree and irreverent, risking the possibility of being seen as brash, or even crude.

Boats feature prominently in both novel and film, set for the most part in Italy. Dickie's boat *Bird* is a prized possession, and perhaps the one exception to the rule about his lack of interest in material things. Crucially, though, the appeal of the boat is the lifestyle that it affords Dickie, and his ability to host lavish excursions for the friends who drop by to see him – this is not a Rolex watch or a Chippendale desk bought from Sotheby's. In fact, Dickie's life of constant movement actively spurns the ownership of large items: it is the freedom that he most treasures, and it is the freedom that is also the most telling about his position in life. By contrast, Dickie's father is a shipping magnate whose wealth is nevertheless tied to ongoing and ceaseless 'work' of a kind, albeit still highly exploitative and degrading of other people. In this respect, the older Greenleaf represents a more primitive and not-so-untethered form of wealth than his son, and it is this contrast that explains the tension which exists between them, as it does between the different generations of so many wealthy families.

The Talented Mr Ripley is really a story, then, about the differences in how people move through the world – the lack of resistance felt by those who have money, and the scheming that is required of those who don't. What is casual and a given to those on top, becomes aspirational and a point of fixation to those underneath. As Dickie Greenleaf represents a sort of acme or peak of prosperity – a man so rich he can treat money and the people supplying it with total disdain – then it stands to reason that Tom Ripley, and people like him, would aspire not to own grand palaces and jewellery, but to experience a total ease of movement, and the ability to do nothing but pursue adventure and novelty. With time being the greatest luxury of all, and where we have seen this play out in a desire for objects that show the visible traces of having been produced slowly and with care, the ultimate expression of prosperity perhaps removes the need for objects altogether. It is the demonstration of having no responsibility, of being separate from the world of work and material concern altogether.

Yet in the way that synthetic, mass-produced and even virtual versions can be made of rustic objects, these dupes can also exist in the world of activity. In fact, the experience economy as a whole might be considered a dupe of the life that is enjoyed by the leisure class, and an attempt to create synthetic, bite-sized alternatives that allow participants to project a degree of prosperity to the outside world. The truism that there is no better way of spending your money than on creating memories – which in the popular sense refers to novelty, rather than memories of the kind associated with deep, emotional connection, communal endeavour, or the private communion between the self and a nice poem, for example – is one that is used to feed an industry of ever-more obscure and commoditised encounters: rapid-fire, week-long food tours of whole countries; introduction courses to age-old traditions; seeing the world from alternative vantage points – above, below, from a hovercraft; eating in the dark; vespa riding; Segway riding; seeing the Italian coast from a vintage Fiat 500 for £500; eating from a table suspended one hundred feet above ground. The list is endless; and as the supply increases, integrity diminishes. The difference between my friend and I boarding a yacht in the South of France and Dickie Greenleaf boarding his, is that Greenleaf really had the time to perfect the art of sailing. We, on the other hand, relied on the services of a man who had understandably taken advantage of an emerging market, and one that had few checks and balances in place.

The other relevant aspect of the novel is its setting in the 1950s and its treatment of the emerging technology and apparatus on which the experience economy relies. *The Talented Mr Ripley* is one of five novels in a series, all of which deal in aspects of globalisation, including international travel and an international banking system. Characters are frequently cashing international cheques, wiring money and hiring places to live, in what was still a relatively new phenomenon that marked a point of departure from the more stuffy and parochial forms of high society that had predominated in the nineteenth century, centred around small social circles whose interactions were confined to highly orchestrated events, and often those set by tradition. The second novel in the series, *Ripley Under Ground*, was published in 1970, fifteen years after the first, at a time when commercial air-travel was well-established and starting to boom. The opportunities for constant transformation, multiple lives lived in multiple places, and an identity that was free to be much more elusive on account of being untethered from its immediate surroundings, were all conditions that Highsmith exploited in her continuing tales of deception and forgery. As a queer woman who spent much of her life in Vienna, she also evidently celebrated these conditions, and rightly acknowledged them as offering escape from the bigotry and prejudices that had also characterised smaller communities.

Tom Ripley seizes on these new opportunities, but has none of the worldliness with which to take it in his stride. With the opening up of so much travel and exposure to different cultures, came the suggestion that everyone was free to be an adventurer, and that money spent in this vein might constitute something more noble than all of the tasteful consumer goods combined. But for those without recourse to family wealth or a health insurance plan, the idea of being intrepid didn't always land. This recalls a conversation I had when I was a student, after making my friends come to the cinema to watch the documentary film *Man on Wire* (dir., James Marsh, 2008), centred on the life of tightrope walker and stuntman Philippe Petit, and with particular focus on the preparation and execution of Petit's forty-five-minute performance on a rope suspended between the World Trade Center towers in 1974. Crossing the wire eight times in total, Petit walked, danced, knelt and lay suspended 1,350 feet above the New York streets, claiming after the event that he could hear the sound of muttering and cheering from the people who were stood on the ground below. It remains a staggering spectacle, and Petit is deserving of his many accolades for testing the bounds of human achievement, and what might be possible through the accomplishment of skill, not to mention the overcoming of fear.

I have always been interested by extremity, and what compels human beings to pursue outlandish feats that defy all rules of safety and good reason. I am not particularly brave and have never felt the compulsion to throw myself out of a plane or from a suspended platform on a bungee rope, but I am fascinated by people who do, and the motivations that drive them. It was this that my friends and I discussed on our walk back from watching the film: whether Petit had ever seriously considered the possibility of death, what it must have felt like, and if he was ever able to achieve the same rush or sense of achievement again. One friend, however, remained quiet, waiting until we had almost reached home to tell us that far from liking the film she believed what Petit had done was irresponsible and showed little concern for the people who loved him.

'What about his children?' she said.

'I'm not sure he has children,' I replied.

'What if he did?'

What seemed ridiculous to me, then – and which I responded to by telling my friend that she was missing the point, that there was a separation between the artist and their work – has started to seem more legitimate over time. It is not insignificant that this person was also the poorest among our group of friends – the daughter of a bin collector who had been raised in a one-bedroom flat in the suburb of Romford, Essex, on the outskirts of London. I don't say this patronisingly, or to insinuate that such an experience had in any way mired her judgement, only to state that due to personal circumstances, her priorities were always much more practical than those of her peers, due to a huge burden of responsibility that she felt to rectify her family's financial hardship. That no such burden ever worried me is really a reflection of my selfishness rather than any enormous comparative advantages of wealth and prosperity, but I am ashamed to say that I occasionally joined in with my peers when they gently mocked her enjoyment of novelty shot-glass holders, and frozen Chinese platters from the supermarket chain Iceland, for example – directed by a somewhat pathetic desire to fit in. This was also the context in which we seemed to judge her response to the film, which we saw as provincial and lacking any serious understanding of the arts; and it was hypocritical, because despite what we said, all of us actually harboured some desire to live in a state of absolute comfort and would certainly never have been willing to take any kind of physical risk ourselves.

This became the central dilemma of my early twenties, in fact, as I yearned for a comfort that would have been redemptive and helped to cure some of my more anxious tendencies, while also feeling compelled to fulfil a popular expectation that young people should be bold, take risks, see the world. In *Man on Wire* Petit even tells us, 'life should be lived on the edge' and to 'see every day as a true challenge', but this film was hardly the sole cause of my anxious obligations, as similar adages could be found almost everywhere, spurred on by a vast industry of gap-year travel, activity-based holidays, and the re-emergence of gonzo-style journalism being popularised by companies such as VICE. This was also the time that the 'bucket list' entered the common language, and the idea that each of us should have a list of goals to fulfil before being taken by the cold hand of death. Dating apps seemed to be flooded with people declaring the number of countries they had visited, like nineteenth-century frontiersmen proudly announcing their conquests and with photos to prove it. This was the age of corporate festivals and a competition to advertise an ability to endure unhygienic conditions and stay up for nights on end. I did some of this – bar the gap year and the gonzo journalism, thankfully – and as such, believed I was fulfilling the higher purpose of my existence – to see, do, hear and taste as much as possible, all the while quietly scoffing at those who reminded me from the sidelines of another way to live.

Where the leisure class met with rampant individualism and the emergence of new technology that enabled everyone to broadcast their own story to the world, there emerged an outlook that differed slightly from the feckless marauding of Dickie Greenleaf, of considering one's life as a finite resource that needed to be 'spent' well. The distinction between 'life' and 'things' had once been much clearer, where 'things' would also include holidays, but conceived of in a way that was nevertheless still patently materialistic – facilitated by new products such as the package holiday, where it became a routine occurrence and also reduced to the sum total of its framed photographs and souvenirs. Growing up, we often had holidays, but they existed as something apart from life, in much the same way that fashion and shopping did. The holiday, in the same way as a new pair of trainers, was a treat and did not constitute life itself – that soft, indistinct and soupy place we occupied from day to day, much like Kechiche captures in the scenes of Adele around the family dinner table with her family. Money was used to punctuate what we considered to be 'life', with exciting detours and the odd beautiful object, whose sole purpose was enjoyment, but not necessarily meaning, or memory.

Much of the popular discourse that seemed to encircle the tourism industry in my early twenties made a commodity of *life* itself, transforming it into something that might be bought, or booked in advance. There is no judgement in the opposing outlooks or worldviews being set up here, only an observation in how consumer attitudes changed, and the adaptations of an industry, to either spur on that change or else respond to it, and cater to the need of everyone seeking to *live life to the max*. If shopping had once constituted an aspect of life to which it was nevertheless considered subordinate, the experience economy had emerged to make a confusing blend of the two.

Acts of betterment

So far this book has detailed the many ways in which the idea of good taste is often informed by the tacit expression of the increasingly precious and rarefied commodity of time. This can be seen in objects that are conspicuously handmade, and thereby indicative of the consumer's ability to purchase another person's time; or in the facilitation of crafts and activities that the consumer themself is able to devote vast amounts of time to, either through the impression of great health and a lengthy skincare regimen that might be demonstrated through 'barely there' cosmetic interventions, or else through food and other such creations that would serve to indicate an interest in culinary craft and skill. The natural end point of this would be to remove material goods altogether, and convey one's ultimate virtue as a consumer – and by proxy, superlative good taste – by becoming a connoisseur of time itself.

A currency of experiences emerges then, with gimmicky at one end and activities aimed at 'improving' us at the other. These activities enhance a person's cultural capital, through their health-giving benefits or the opportunities they offer for showcasing a set of attributes connected to employability. CVs frequently include whole sections in which to list them: marathons, mountain climbing, forms of orienteering or swimming in a cold climate. All of these are capable of boosting a person's employability, and the tendency isn't limited to physical exploits either, but also includes the mastering of a skill, from short-lived cookery courses, to pottery making or painting. Key to observe is the shift from authentic interest to crash course – experiences that can be bought in advance and rounded off with a neat certificate.

Burning Man, the festival held each year in the Nevada Desert and attended by as many as 80,000 people, is one of the world's largest organised festivals and a fitting event to consider in terms of its place within the experience economy. For tech workers living on the West Coast of America, attendance at Burning Man had become almost compulsory by the late 2010s. As attendees are prone to reminding anyone who will listen, it is an event forged out of the countercultural movements that first occurred on that Coast during the 1960s, starting out as a bonfire hosted annually in San Francisco, then moving to the Black Rock desert in Nevada, where its founders Kevin Evans, John Law and Michael Mikel began to expand their ambition. Autonomy was applied as an early principle, inspired by the earlier notion, first coined by the anarchist Hakim Bey, of the temporary autonomous zone. The festival was built around self-directed performances and the practise of subsistence. As it developed, money would be banned and attendees required to trade goods and services in order to get by. That the event was short-lived, though long by most contemporary festival standards – lasting nine days in total – and its lifestyle adjustments therefore virtual, with the possibility for participants to return to 'normality' whenever they liked, Burning Man formed a sort of innocent experiment that theoretically posed no harm or offence to anyone who did not wish to attend. What did start to seem increasingly offensive, in the years that followed, was a soaring attendance fee and a profile of participant that did not so much constitute a wholesale replacement of the former hippy by the corporate shill of the present, but actually that new Frankenstein creation that existed somewhere in the middle of the two: the shoeless, tech-bro 'creative'. Where the utopia of the early tech industry had collided with big money, a new capitalist had been born, convinced of his ability to reconcile the mercenary greed that swelled inside of him, with new technological solutions they claimed to be creating in the interests of everyone. The sanctimony with which Burning Man and its spectacle of an alternative lifestyle was narrated sat uncomfortably with the truth, that it had increasingly become a playground of the inordinately wealthy. Entirely opposed to its foundational ideas of a cash-free idyll, attendees are known to frequently travel to the event in their private jets, import luxury foods and host exclusive events within the larger festival.

The fastest U-turn I have ever performed with respect to a writer was on reading Geoff Dyer's essay in praise of Burning Man in 2003, published four years after he first attended the event in 1999.[3] In the years since, Dyer's enthusiasm for the festival and its many offerings has never waned, and there have been ample opportunities for him to rectify his judgement – to set the record straight, as they say. As recently as 2018, after making a final visit, and against the flood of criticism of the event's elitism and hypocrisy, Dyer was quoted in the *Guardian* as saying it was, 'even more stupendous than when I first went in 1999', and that, 'the quality of art has improved to the extent that Burning Man has left other contemporary art gatherings trailing in its (very dusty) wake'.[4] The art, referred to by Dyer here, and for anyone fortunate enough to have never laid eyes on it, is not art at all but pure capitalist imaginary, untethered from any wider discourse, conversation or notion of art history, not born of study, but a steampunk elephant made of scrap metal, whose locomotive is being powered by two women wearing silver bikinis, the sex-positivity to which they believe themselves a part, somehow centred on very wealthy men hosting sex parties. It constitutes the very extremes of free-flowing corporate stupidity. Only a brain completely addled on Huel and *Final Fantasy* – played at the end of a day spent otherwise staring at a screen – and incapable of anything other than a surface, porny view of reality, could tolerate Burning Man's spectacle of aestheticised progressive sentiment and equality. Beyond its misplaced belief in the integrity of its so-called art, and the enormous carbon footprint, what inspires the strongest aversion towards Burning Man, however, is its insistence on framing mild gestures of a non-existent rebellion as some kind of radical act. It is the assumption made by most attendees that the grand, beautiful, world-altering political and artistic movements of the past might be treated as little more than a costume. And that the application of some accessories inspired by the films of Guillermo del Toro might allow even the most wanton capitalist to savour some of its magic.

Thankfully such an abomination as Burning Man has never found its way onto British shores, and though inevitable comparisons are made with Glastonbury Festival – held most years in Somerset and with a capacity to host over 300,000 people – the festival itself is an event that is nevertheless spared the absurdity of its American counterpart, partly due to a British tendency to always resist earnest sentiment – a drawback in many ways, and one that breeds all kinds of neuroses, but in this one limited sense, proves to be quite useful.

Where this cynicism is lacking in the British context, and where it could afford to be applied, is in an event whose name I can barely bring myself to type, but surely must for the greater good of completing this book. Tough Mudder is a corporatised adventure race in which participants cover a distance of sixteen to nineteen kilometres while simultaneously overcoming a host of physical obstacles inspired by military drills. Much like military training, Tough Mudder combines the marathon experience with aspects of extreme sport, in a challenge meant to test the physical and mental capacities of its participants. Its obstacles are designed to induce fear, and often incorporate some of our most deeply held aversions, such as fire, confined spaces and heights. Tough Mudder is now extremely popular, both with individual participants and groups of friends, but it is also attended by large groups of colleagues on team-building exercises, the international accountancy firm Deloitte being a loyal customer. At time of writing, mention of the adventure programme is even included in the official online Deloitte recruitment website aimed at demonstrating to would-be applicants the full breadth of interests enjoyed by its many, well-rounded and worldly employees.[5]

Part of Tough Mudder's advertising strategy was to have each event exhaustively documented by professional photographers, whose images would be uploaded onto Facebook the following day with a branded watermark. Participants would be tagged in the images, in a model that borrowed heavily from the strategy of club promoters in the years prior. Both an extension of the experience itself – the anticipation and excitement of receiving the images forming part of its overall appeal – and also a badge of honour, these branded images would then be circulated far and wide, as fresh audiences were exposed to this curious new form of weekend activity that was taking corporate Britain by storm.

Bear necessities

Part of this sense that one's life is a finite commodity that needs to be well spent is the drive to also live much more conspicuously. Events like Tough Mudder, but marathons, too, were optimised for sharing and engagement, and employed a whole secondary industry of photographers and social media managers in the service of allowing participants to widely advertise their exploits. It coincided with the appearance on our screens of a person who might be considered the high priest of the experience economy, Bear Grylls: the cold and haughty antonym to the earlier and much more endearing enthusiasm of naturist Steve Irwin, who sadly died when he was stung by a ray. Grylls represented the first and most successful foray into television and light entertainment, of a type that had existed for centuries, the wealthy man preoccupied with survivalism and adventure. It was a preoccupation that had put Edmund Hillary on the top of Mount Everest, but it was also one that had led to the rape and pillage of the

Southern hemisphere, and the subsequent civilising missions that had served to impose British culture on the rest
of the world throughout the nineteenth century. Dislocated
from this wider history, however, Grylls was free to occupy
the public imagination as a modern adventurer, a man who
laughed in the face of danger and frequently drank his own
piss. Press shots would be chiselled and pensive, and the
voiceover to his shows would be accompanied by booming
soundtracks of an action movie variety. Decades of trying to
undo the work of a toxic gender binary that insisted on men's
sole function as practical creatures built to fight – decades
too of trying to urge consumers towards a more plant-based
diet – would be challenged by the presence on our TV screens
of a military propagandist espousing ideas about the purpose
of life being to test our limits and subsist exclusively on
raw steak.[6]

Despite protestations to the contrary (he is always very
keen to stress his aversion to celebrity and fame), Grylls
not only popularised the idea of survivalism, but of docu-
menting that survivalism in the name of a profile. He would
become famous for his first hit TV show, *Man Vs Wild*,
where audiences would be given a course in how to survive
the wilderness. During the series, Grylls would be tasked
with having to forage for food, kill live animals, traverse
open ravines and dive into unknown waters. That the show
has since been criticised, with several journalists finding
evidence that Grylls on occasion slept in the relative comfort
of a nearby hotel and was supplied food via the show's crew,
will not be news to most, and it hardly interests me either,
compared to the show's spectacle (although it does reinforce

the fact of it being just that), why it was so popular and what it could tell us about the society in which it was created. *Man Vs Wild* first aired in 2006, and over a year before the world endured the financial shock of the 2008 market crash. The broadly liberal, relatively prosperous era of American – and by proxy, Western – growth was still very much upon us. As such, matters of survival were still confined to the realm of the imaginary, and able to amuse us in their unlikelihood. During this time, Grylls was always billed as an 'adventurer' in a term that came complete with associations of superfluity and anomaly status – of being compelled to do things for the sake of it, that more sane-minded and reasonable people would avoid.[7]

Over time, however, Grylls became known more as a survivalist; and for audiences, the teachings in his shows started to assume a greater urgency, perhaps as we were being confronted with the possibility of our own financial hardship, not to mention the collapse of global ecosystems whose effects were becoming ever more frequent and visible. In 2010 Grylls collaborated with commercial knife manufacturer Gerber, producing a range of sheath knives and multitool devices, firestarters and scout blades that proved popular and have since become something of a staple among gardening, DIY and camping enthusiasts. Grylls's wisdom was also shared in a series of self-help books combining experience gleaned from survival missions and extreme challenges, and pseudo-spiritual fare of the kind associated with figures like Eckhart Tolle, or Oprah. These included *Soul Fuel* (2021) and *Mind Fuel* (2022) – a somewhat more traditionally masculine and less sentimental version of the familiar 'soul food' or 'mind food', presumably – *How to Stay Alive* (2017), *Never Give Up* (2021), *A Survival Guide to Life* (2012), *Mud Sweat and Tears* (2011), and *Facing Up: A Remarkable Journey to the Summit of Mount Everest* (2009), not to mention a long list of books seemingly aimed at younger readers and appearing like a more modern reworking of the traditional 'boy's own' survival tales.

Meanwhile, joining Grylls in the expansion of this rapidly growing empire of associated products and goods to survive the coming end times, were a host of celebrities keen to test (and of course, display) their own strength of character and fitness. This celebrity-focused iteration of the Grylls entertainment ecosystem was called *Running Wild with Bear Grylls* and featured as far-reaching celebrity guests as Channing Tatum, Will Ferrell, Kate Winslet, former Spice Girl Mel B, Natalie Portman and, most famously, then president of the United States, Barack Obama. In addition to the Obama episode's ostensible purpose of showing people the real-world effects of climate change on the geological landscape of the Alaskan wilderness, was an opportunity to reinforce Obama's public image as a cool guy. At the beginning of the episode, Obama admits that it is the first time he has ever been able to freely wander around Alaska, being otherwise confined to its airbase, and stresses that most other days are spent in the stuffy environs of his office, where it is mandatory to wear a suit and tie.

In that same episode, Grylls takes the rather unexpected step of asking the president if he can say a prayer for him – a request that Obama agrees to. Obama then proceeds to be blessed by the TV show presenter in what is possibly, beyond all instances of bravery and intrepidity, the strongest indication of Grylls's preternatural, almost psychopathic confidence, as he then lays a hand on the president's shoulder and proceeds to implore god on high to protect him. If Obama had hoped to provide the American public an entertaining segment with insight into his character and a side-order of climate change awareness, then they also got a lesson in the awkwardness created by people who are unable to read social cues.

The Obama episode was nevertheless a hit, cementing both men's reputations in the other's domain – Obama would close off his double tenure as president with macho credentials intact, if not boosted, while Grylls would be able to posit himself more convincingly as a wellness coach and mindfulness influencer. A tacit connection had been drawn between experience, self-imposed hardship and austerity, moral virtue and faith, and it would be one that ran into the subject of Grylls's writing, speeches and interviews thereafter. In a documentary with Louis Theroux in 2022, Grylls made the unexpected admission that his mother had enjoyed taking him to see motivational speakers as a child, such as Tim Robbins and Zig Ziglar. He also shared several motivational adages, such as 'pick the road less travelled' and 'face your fears'.

So much of what is considered to be tasteful has been touched by the survivalist mentality, appearing earthen and natural, even when its methods of production are synthetic and exploitative, or when its price point is prohibitively expensive. But this also extends to the physical environments endorsed by so much modern branding, such as those adopted by Pattern and the modern travel company, such as Airbnb, of sunsets and Chinese sky lanterns floating off into the distance, friends running naked into vast lakes, and hidden campsites miraculously surrounded by festoon lighting. The very idea of Hygge, a trend that first originated in Scandinavia and became popular globally in the late 2010s, is based on the concept of a retreat from modernity. This was not comfort of the sterile, labour-saving kind that had meant safety and security in the past, and which came complete with in-home entertainment and mod-cons, but a comfort that was based on the idea of escaping such entrapments, and finding a warm nook in a log cabin or lakeside boathouse.

In an article published by the *New Yorker* on the subject in 2016, Hygge was defined as, 'a quality of cosiness and comfortable conviviality that engenders a feeling of contentment or wellbeing'.[8] What it meant for adopters outside of Denmark and Norway, however, was also affecting the atmosphere of a small village in the far northern hemisphere – and what cosiness and comfortable conviviality might mean there, specifically; a fantasy of stacked logs and wood-burner stoves, sofas weighed down by 100-per-cent yak-wool blankets, shag rugs and hurricane lanterns and maybe even mounted antlers, wholly coherent with rural Sweden perhaps, but somewhat superfluous in suburban Greater Manchester. Since then, other pretenders to Hygge have included Mys, synonymous with Hygge and equivalent to the word 'cosy' in English; Lagom, translatable to 'just what's right', which in real terms amounts to a slightly more minimal variation on the first (of a Hygge with slightly fewer accoutrements and considerably more white); as well as Fika, the trend inherited from Swedish tradition, of enjoying baked goods and coffee in the middle of the working afternoon.

In each case, however, these traditions are adopted for their aesthetic, while discounting any consideration of social and cultural history. A flattering nod to Scandinavian culture on one hand, but perhaps also a crude and cartoonish projection of what an external audience perceives Scandinavian culture to be through only the most tired and overplayed of clichés. These trends nevertheless had the Western tourism industry in a chokehold, as every Airbnb rental and hotel devoted itself to the fantasy of the timber merchant's nightly fireside vigil, while many of us paid hundreds of pounds per night for the privilege of sharing in its restorative wealth. Thus the retreat, as opposed to the more traditional 'stay' or 'weekend break' was invented, which was no longer required to merely fulfil an expectation of cleanliness or even opulence, but to signal 'escape' through its inclusion of so many romantic tropes inherited from pop culture and mainstream entertainment.

It begged the question of what we were all escaping from. If holidays had once been sold to us as products in the pages of brochures, with smiling, modelesque families presented as a sort of life in Technicolor, then in the years since, they had been reimagined as sites of recoil, where the modern world might be excluded for the purposes of facilitating a more essential experience. Bear Grylls and the Hygge homestay might seem worlds apart in terms of their objectives, both harnessed popular psychology connected with resourcefulness and wellbeing to sell us different parts of the same story: the intrepid adventure and the homely haven to be found at its end. In addition to Hygge, Mys, Lagom and Fika, there had also been an attempt to mount a popular interest in Sisu, a Finnish concept of resilience, determination and staying power. What became the subject of a thousand inspirational coffee mugs, wall hangings, candles and reed diffusers, differed only in spelling from the ideas espoused by Grylls in his many books. Could the tourism industry, by adapting to the mindset of its consumers and supplying images of the wilderness – be it in raw detail, or held at bay beyond the boundary of the wood lodge or the bothy – be reflecting back to us the nature of our own fears? Had the reality of recurring economic crises and the imminent threat posed by climate change created a desire to deny modern life altogether, and perhaps even acquire skills for the reality that lay beyond the horizon of its collapse through a synthetic and mass-produced luddism? Was the experience economy a way of gamifying our despair, and of trying to find novelty value in the dependency on our own resources for survival: escape rooms, eating in the dark, paid-for foraging sprees, to name but a few?

If, in other areas of life, the idea of taste had become inextricable from the idea of resourcefulness, then the same would apply to experience, due to what seemed to be a growing sense of doom and awareness for our collective mortality. Anything that constituted a waste of time would be considered tasteless, while anything that could proffer a benefit – be it connected to wellbeing, education or the creation of 'new memories' (a currency that seemed to now dictate everything we did) – would emerge as a new form of luxury. In the transformation of *leisure* into *experience*, there was a requirement to be in some way improving or memorable, which – much like the discussion surrounding popular trends in food – failed to acknowledge the necessity of its earlier and more traditional definitions, where it had been connected to fun and the relinquishing of professional responsibility for those who were heavily burdened by their labour. The ability to devote one's spare time to the pursuit of refining activities that might improve the mind, body, spirit or Instagram feed is, once again, overlooked as being the luxury of those working reasonable hours in relatively non-strenuous environments.

The right sort of leisure can trump all other forms of tasteful expression. A chic home, understated fashions, natural beauty and an ability to rustle up healthy fare, all pale in comparison to being well-travelled and not even conversant in a variety of cultures, but rich in a stock of photos acquired from visiting those cultures. This is the ultimate use of time and money, so says the popular wisdom, above fun or laughter or play or sleep, to the extent that we are often made to feel guilty for using our time in ways that serve no purpose beyond instant gratification and a sense of play. In the insistence that everyone now devote their spare time to the ticking off of a bucket list that is mandatory, is the denial of drudgery and hardship. It is the condemnation of merely going out, sunbathing, walking aimlessly, sitting in the park, reading for hours or staring at the sky.

Image masters

I have toyed with discussing the following two cases at different places throughout this book – relevant as they are to fashion, beauty and food – but chose ultimately to discuss them here, at the end of the book, due to what they can tell us about the value systems that govern our reality. When appearances reign supreme, the winners are increasingly those who display the prowess of the connoisseur. Differing, crucially, from the expert or the maestro – those who are studied in a particular field and possesses the wisdom of a specific school or applied craft – the connoisseur is merely adept at reading and responding to particular trends and shifts in power relations between people, such that they remain at the cutting edge of whatever is deemed to be respectable and approved of as 'good taste'.

The first of these cases has become an icon of the age, a Mona Lisa of the influencer era, if you will. The centuries of exaggerated hype, mystique and conspiracy theory that compel visitors to pile in by the millions every year to the Louvre and gawp at Leonardo da Vinci's original painting is partly driven by the depicted figure's defiance of any neat categorisation. Society not being content with having policed the female body for millennia, and the quantities of flesh it might be permitted to reveal, an adjunct theory – that feminine intrigue might be enhanced through the obscuring of any discernible emotion – evolved alongside. The archaic smile, the name given to the tendency in Greek sculpture to create a smile that was so subtle and so lifelike as to suggest the possibility of an actual sentience, was one that da Vinci applied to his subject. In that context, however, and in an age of Christianity with its distillation of womanhood into either Madonna or whore, the effect would mesmerise audiences for its lifelike proportions but also for its confounding ambiguity, and the suggestion that an otherwise pious woman could also contain the potential for chaos. Five centuries later it is why we are still gawping at the painting as well as any other spectacle of womanhood that evades the simple categorisation of either perfect victim or villain, in the widely circulated celebrity mugshot, paparazzi or courtroom photograph. Such images have become so widely circulated, so picked apart and pored over, as to define a whole era of celebrity pop culture and news reporting, as the world asks: *Are they on drugs? Did someone abuse them? What went wrong?* Turn your mind to the image of Britney Spears enduring a fairly understandable rebellion and rejection of the male gaze, or Lindsay Lohan's personal affront to the pervy dads of the world by evolving past its expectations as the impish tyke of Disney movies *Freaky Friday* (1976, et al) and *The Parent Trap* (1961). But none inspires this incredulity more so than Anna Sorokin, the fake heiress who attracted the world's attention, and prompted a million column inches, when she was charged with defrauding acquaintances and investors out of thousands of dollars of cash; who, more so than anyone else mentioned in this book, demonstrated the true heights of frenzy that our culture's preoccupation with taste and image had reached.

Being young and a woman, and therefore, by implication, guileless, acquiescent and eager to please, Sorokin baffled the world by not fitting the traditional profile of a fraudster. In interviews from prison following her later conviction, Sorokin boldly affirmed that she is 'not a good person', because after all, who can confidently say that they are? It was for all these reasons that pictures of her became inescapable, coolly staring out from behind oversized glasses, sometimes appearing to frown, other times turning over her shoulder to smile at an acquaintance in the courtroom. Throughout the trial, Sorokin's outfits were analysed and dissected, though they usually consisted of babydoll dresses – one black, one white, one snakeskin – a choker and ballet pumps. It is perhaps no surprise that given the unlikely events of her case, combined with the short skirt and steely refusal to express emotion, Sorokin – or at least her image – provided a sort of manna to the Internet with its bottomless appetite for the perplexing. As such, and since her release from prison in early 2021, Sorokin has become a totem, her image likely to become as synonymous with the age as Patty Hearst holding an assault rifle is to the 1970s.

Sorokin's story is one that deals in deception, the dynamics of modern celebrity, PR and self-promotion, and the enormous pitfalls in a system of abstracted capital and credit. But it is mainly the story of how one woman seized on the clownish status anxiety that exists with respect to matters of connoisseurship, insider knowledge, experience, image and good taste, as Sorokin skilfully navigated an art and fashion world whose entire currency is centred on manners and matters of aesthetic judgement.

Born in Russia and later moving to Germany with her family, the Anna Sorokin story begins with a move to study at the art school Central Saint Martins in London, alma mater of Alexander McQueen, Stella McCartney and Gilbert & George. We can assume from this information that Sorokin possessed at least a basic gift for design. Sorokin never enrolled, however, briefly returning to Germany after a short stay in London, where she worked for a PR firm. Soon after which she would arrive in Paris and begin an internship at the French fashion magazine, *Purple*.

It was here that Sorokin seems to have forged her fake identity, Anna Delvey. If Sorokin's father had worked as a truck driver and her mother had run a local convenience store, then Delvey's father presided over a €60 million overseas trust fund that she would use to leverage favours from wealthy friends. According to a *New York Times* profile: 'Jurors heard evidence that Ms Sorokin tricked a close friend into paying for her and two others to take a luxury vacation in Morocco, talked City National Bank into forking over $100,000 and persuaded the executive of a private jet company to let her fly on credit. She also ran up large tabs at luxury hotels and restaurants that she never paid.'⁹

At the height of her deception, Sorokin had almost successfully persuaded investors to lease her the historic Church Missions House on Park Avenue in New York on the basis of installing an arts foundation and gallery space. She had enlisted the help of Gabriel Andres Calatrava, son of the famous Spanish architect Santiago Calatrava to help redesign the space. According to the *New York Times* profile: 'The younger Calatrava testified that he was trying to build his portfolio when Ms. Sorokin told him of her plans to open a private club called ADF, for the Anna Delvey Foundation. She said it would be similar to Soho House New York with a bar, a nightclub and an art exhibit. He agreed to design it [...] Mr Calatrava said Ms. Sorokin settled on 281 Park Avenue South as the site of her club – a six-story [sic] New York City landmark building with a copper and terracotta roof, marble mosaic floors and stained glass windows. The project was to cost up to $40 million. She began negotiations with the landlord, while her lawyer at the time, Andrew Lance, sought financial assistance from hedge funds and banks, prosecutors said. One bank, City National, had already turned down Ms. Sorokin's request for a $22 million loan when a banker there could not determine the source of her wealth ...' [10]

Sorokin's ascent hinged on her ability to perfect certain mannerisms and modes of taste. Navigating the worlds of investment finance, fashion and art in New York, Paris and London didn't just require the insinuation of wealth, but the demonstration of cultural capital. Or, to put it more accurately, the demonstration of cultural capital insulated the lie, providing an added barrier of defence against potential scepticism and distrust. Delvey presented as a European dilettante, demonstrating an introductory knowledge of music, fashion, literature and fine art. Her Instagram feed resembled that of countless influencers and social media celebrities, with a neat balance of aeroplane window shots, cultural references (the odd Barbara Kruger work, the occasional photo of proto-influencer Jane Birkin and her 'boyfriend' Serge Gainsbourg), incidental mood shots of hazy sunsets, empty tennis courts and rain, the New York skyline, the Paris skyline, some raw vegetables placed artfully on a chopping board, large white boxes with the names of various fashion brands printed on them in ebony sans-serif fonts, Agnes Martin paintings, seagulls, feet. As the profile reports from her ill-fated trip to Morocco, in which Sorokin's failure to provide a functioning credit card to pay for the luxury hotel they had been staying at would ultimately precipitate her demise: 'It was late on Monday afternoon, after almost two full days in La Mamounia's walled palace. It was time to venture out. Anna wanted two things: piles of spices worthy of an Instagram photo and a place to buy some Moroccan kaftans.'[11]

Anna Sorokin fascinates us on the one hand due to the extremity of her story – the conviction, the self-belief and commitment to a false identity that would seem unfathomable to most of us. But she also fascinates for being so quintessentially *of the age*, with its emphasis on vanity. Anna Sorokin is perhaps the most vivid incarnation yet of a tendency that has been facilitated – even, perhaps, necessitated – by the total supplanting of reality by appearances, where not even repeat reminders of reality – such as having your credit card declined, or continually failing to come good on debts – can ultimately uproot your status or cachet. The Instagram follower count, the phone book contacts, the PR connections, the gifted offerings from luxury brands, the comprehensive knowledge of every menu and every wine list in New York, the knowledge of Serge Gainsbourg and Jane Birkin, the ability to dash off the names of renowned architects or writers without having any real, thorough knowledge of their work, the knowledge that a Supreme hoodie and yoga pants pays higher dividends than a Celine overcoat (under the right circumstances, and the knowledge that certain circumstances *call for* the Celine overcoat) all testify to it. Regardless of the lies, the debts she accrued along the way, even regardless of the resulting prison stint, Anna Sorokin is now a somebody, and that cannot be taken away. At the time of writing, she has recently delivered talks to students at Harvard Business School, sold $340,000 from selling her paintings and drawings, and is apparently signed up to work on a new docuseries (following on from the success of the fictionalised account of

Sorokin's story 'Inventing Anna', hosted by Netflix, a project that she was not involved in).[12]

Which brings us to the documentary *Sour Grapes* (2016), and the story of Rudy Kurniawan, who was released in 2020 after serving six years of a ten-year prison sentence after becoming the first man in American history to be charged with the crime of wine fraud. Peddling counterfeit wine mixed in his kitchen sink, the Indonesian Kurniawan, established himself as something of a rebel in a world dominated by old-boy networks and established wealth. He is reputed to have sold up to $24.7 million worth of wine per auction, so that by the time he was caught, the number of fake bottles shifted was believed to have reached 12,000. Among his victims were writer Jay McInerney as well as the billionaire businessman Bill Koch.

The mainstay of Kurniawan's client base, however, was in northern California, with its concentration of money-to-burn tech workers and the crew-neck capitalists for whom connoisseurship was paramount to the projected image of nonchalant erudition. Wine, it becomes apparent throughout *Sour Grapes*, is one reliable investment for the conveyance of both wealth and cultural capital: as a finite, depleting commodity, its monetary value is staggering – the right vintage from 1945 can now fetch over half a million dollars – but beyond that is a Dickie Greenleaf level of worldly erudition. For Kurniawan's clients it wasn't enough to be rich, one also had to display the superlative judgement, a refined palate and a rarefied experience. Even after being swindled, Koch proudly shows the documentary's cameraman his collection of 'impressionistic' (sic) paintings, Samurai swords, and

Greco-Roman statue replicas, in what looks like a slightly outdated, Trumpian effort to achieve the same aims as his younger acquaintances. At the point where wine culture collides with unabated capitalism, the results are distorted and clownish, the original point of fascination blown out of all proportion as Koch leads us through a theme park of wine collecting, where the wine cellar boasts replica medieval chandeliers and the toilet's walls are inlaid with the carcasses of wine bottles past.

Kurniawan's enterprise crashed the price of wine collections around the world, publicly humiliating some of the greediest profiteers of human exploitation and exposing the sham that underpins their billion-dollar hobby. It also exposed the ethical limitations of a criminal justice system in which endemic low pay and dehumanising work conditions are valid, while isolated incidents of opportunism and exploitation of the rich are dealt an iron fist. Kurniawan did not share Sorokin's fortune, and instead served seven years in prison before being repatriated to Indonesia upon his release. What unites both stories beyond their scammer tagline however, is that they make only slight re-adjustment of the rules that are stipulated by two industries governed by hot air, deception, price-fixing, and showmanship. Sorokin and Kurniawan's crime was only that they obeyed the law of appearances all too well. In an economy governed by image and demonstrations of taste, their stories cannot be considered anomalous or divergent, but rather, exemplary.

Chapter Seven

Abundance

Only the useful and the beautiful
(or that which sparks joy)
Look in the mirror and take one thing off
Less is more
Good, simple, honest
You can't take it with you

The idea of good vs bad taste, at least by popular definition, is created by the reflex to judge all decisions according to their proficiency in decoding a set of very particular rules. This is a mistake, if not an outright delusion, that ignores the complex and material conditions that inform the consumer habits of people pushed to their absolute limit by a system of degrading capitalism, not to mention denying the existence of cultural strains and visual codes that might exist outside of our immediate experience or awareness. To subscribe to those rules with any kind of seriousness is also to believe in the inherent superiority of one cultural experience (yours) above another (theirs); and to use those rules as grounds to justify remunerating some, and impoverishing others, is to become complicit in that degrading system. It is not an outright agent and propagandist of it.

Capitalism is a system that operates by the illusion of scarcity. Despite there being more than enough housing, food and resources for everyone on earth to live with dignity and comfort, a privileged minority hoards these resources, imposing false limitations that make the majority dependent on them to survive, and as they extract ever-greater profits. At the beginning of this book, I discussed the complications with defining class in an age of large corporations, the service economy, the casualisation of work and rentier capitalism. But the present age is no less afflicted by the greed and cruelty of the wealthy than the nineteenth century was by landowners and factory owners, whose modern-day equivalents are the corporate tech CEOs, shareholders and buy-to-let landlords. Capitalism also evolved past land and goods, and with the help of the advertising industry and new media technology, has encroached on, and commoditised, the more abstract and experiential, such that our free leisure time, our relationships, and even our most basic desires are presented to us as finite and in short supply. We came to see love as being only available to those who fulfilled a very narrow view of beauty that was always waning, and life itself as nothing more than a depleting amount of time that must be 'spent well' – a judgement that was always being measured against the urgency of death: the *one hundred places to visit before you die* approach taken by the modern tourism industry. The idea of scarcity was something that started to pervade our emotional realities, and to avoid the accusation that we might be demanding more than we deserve, working people learned to be unassuming and to repressing their desires and need for self-expression and freedom. Competency in doing so would be praised, and once the financial rewards were understood, this tendency also became competitive, leading to farcical and minute fixations.

Much of what passes for good taste in the current climate, can be read as a way of justifying the logic of scarcity, making it seem beautiful, even aspirational. Conforming to these aesthetic codes signals complicity in this illusion of capitalism and its game; and it is here that the aphorisms listed above come in to play. The pursuit of taste, which is connected to restraint, becomes a necessity of almost anyone reliant on wage labour – a way of indicating that you will not challenge the current order and the mythology that it has created in order to protect itself. These rules are often passed between friends, or parroted on TV shows and on social media, and they make an enemy of excess and chaos – characteristics that signal vanity, greed and an overspill of desire, supposedly. In a climate of rampant over-production, mass consumerism and a huge amount of waste that is destroying the planet and degrading every form of life that it contains, we might be forgiven for thinking that the modesty implied by these statements represents a noble alternative. But what's driving that ecological decline isn't the consumer forced to buy cheap and buy fast, or the person who enjoys accumulating things and making their home busy with stuff, but the vast oversized consumption of the super wealthy, the large corporations that they own, which prevent normal people from accessing the things that they need and making them dependent on mass-market offerings, and the huge surplus models that lead to so much waste. Good taste, by contrast, finds new ways to justify the inequality that it also quietly promotes, incorporating the language of sustainability, good health and responsibility in ways that often distract us from the corporate forces at play.

This is at least the case at the moment. While certain ideas about modesty tend to endure as symbols of respectability and good taste, trends do change, and the varieties of taste will tend to alternate and resist whatever went immediately before. This is why the answer does not lie in seeking to promote alternative modes of taste – be those loud or garish, or fetishizing the working class in ways that are cartoonish, nostalgic and trite. Not only does this serve to caricature and denigrate working people in ways that play into the hands of right-wing despots, it also creates fresh forms of consumer desire, which by their very nature must always seek supremacy and eventually require approval and adoption by the most powerful.

What is important to note, is that whatever the pervasive and popular notion of taste might be at any given time, it is always presented as absolute and unassailable. The statements included at the beginning of each chapter present as universal truths, or attach themselves to ideals that would seem to be the same for everybody on earth: ideas about joy and beauty, but also simplicity and reason. Whether it be the aristocracy of the eighteenth century, the industrialist of the nineteenth century, the entrepreneur and businessman of the twentieth century or the tech person and marketing influencer of the early twenty-first century, the truism will reflect the conditions needed for the working person to accept subjugation, and to censor their own desires. By mistaking these aesthetic preferences, which are manufactured and handed down, for some kind of moral virtue, we justify the interests of the most powerful and allow their dominance to seem inevitable, perhaps even God-given. In addition to the cruelty of financial hardship, this compounds class-based insecurity, low self-esteem and continual consumer anxiety. But more profound than that is the way in which the process naturalises forms of inequality and discrimination. In this respect, discussion surrounding questions of taste often mirrors that of scripture, and perhaps in a secular society governed by consumer behaviours, taste really does constitute a religion of sorts. As a belief system, it suggests a hierarchy of virtue with respect to consumer choices, but it also defers those consumer choices to a force that would seem to be incontestable – one that cannot be challenged on the grounds of subjectivity or bias. By its logic, those with good taste are more deserving than those without; a catch-22 in which it is often the tacit demonstration of free leisure time and the ability to remain abreast of the fast-moving values and beliefs that the tasteful hold, that also determines a person's worthiness of financial security. As such, the idea of taste makes the haves, with their artful grasp of what looks or appears 'good', seem inherently more deserving than the have-nots.

Under the influence of that visual economy, everything that we know has been made facile, and material reality in its entirety reduced to a question of discernment. We see this vividly in the nomenclature that has evolved alongside this new technology; in the transformation of 'homes' into 'spaces', 'clothes' into 'looks', 'cosmetics' into 'beauty', 'food' into 'eats' and 'leisure' into 'experience'. There is a shift from the material to the sensory and virtual. We see this too in the reframing of events that might have once been seen to have real world consequences, into matters of poor aesthetic judgement: the tendency to describe actual racist remarks uttered by politicians and having the effect of legitimising the dehumanisation of millions of people, as matters of 'bad taste'.[1] The disbelief with which we watched the ascent of Donald Trump was one that can be viewed as our cognitive faculties adjusting to the wholesale takeover of the spectacle, where nothing seemed to be real or to have any real-world consequences anymore.

As stated, imminent climate catastrophe and an emphasis on sustainability are being aestheticised too. While relinquishing certain aspects of a synthetic modernity will of course mean having to forgo much that is lurid and loud, oftentimes there is a problem of mistaking the symbolic for the functional. A language of resourcefulness and economy is able to be used in the current moment to justify a tendency that far predates the revival of interest in production methods and sustainability, and actually risks undermining both. The subtext to the statements or truisms listed above, is not that the person on the receiving end must abstain from spending and accruing altogether, but that they must simply redirect their urges towards consumer choices that conform more closely to a very particular aesthetic standard. One great example of this is the current vogue for cotton. Despite experts on the subject being insistent that the energy and water consumption involved in cotton production presents as much of an environmental concern as the decomposition rate of synthetic fibres, the plain white T-shirt signals a degree of responsibility and ethical consumption far above many alternatives. Environmentalism suffers from the gamification involved in trying to recreate a more rustic ideal, which appeals to a highly coveted sense of rural living and tradition.

In nearly all of the examples cited throughout this book, it would seem that we are being recommended to abstain, when in reality these sentiments have either been uttered by people who were selling us products, or else doing the same for a consumer culture that has become highly sophisticated in its methods of marketing. Achieving any one of the pared-back and simple ideals that tastefulness dictates, invariably involves the buying of additional products, be it in the form of new storage solutions or coordinated furnishings, expensive, well-made clothes requiring no further embellishment, beauty products that create the appearance of a 'natural glow' that does not require makeup, health foods and supplements that might transform us from the inside out, or pre-packaged experiences and excursions that promise to deliver something more profound and revelatory than material possession, regardless of their carbon footprint.

The great socialist reformer William Morris might have first intended to bring beauty and dignity to the lives of working people. But his appropriation by mass-market stores, meant he has been reduced to an influencer whose words are taken to justify the very thing that he opposed: poorer people being unable to access beauty, abundance and aesthetic pleasure. He would probably have winced at the way in which his popular designs have been reproduced and sold in large stores like John Lewis at a price that would exclude most working people.

Coco Chanel might not have personally authored the current brand of cartoonish wealth that her eponymous fashion label has since become, but she was nevertheless a salesperson who traded primarily with the wealthy industrialist and aristocrat. Marie Kondo has sold her philosophy of minimal clutter, dubbed the KonMari method, to a tune of several million dollars, despite having personally abandoned the approach herself following the birth of her first child. 'My home is messy,' she told the *Washington Post* in 2023, after years of lecturing the rest of us about the slovenliness with which we supposedly conducted our lives, '[...] but the way I am spending my time is the right way for me at this time at this stage of my life.'[2]

The truth is that our world swirls with stuff, and we cannot save it with the current systems of capital in place. Shifts in consumer habit alone will not save it. As long as we uphold the logic of consumerism, contribute to a culture of aspiration and consumer desire, and as long as our lives are centred around perfecting the art of shopping, styling ourselves or perpetuating a certain lifestyle – the project of living in a perfect home, comprised of seemingly sustainable finishes and furnishings, building a perfect wardrobe composed of so-called ethical fashions – we will be playing our part to keep those old systems alive. If we did want to make adjustments towards a better, collective reality, it would require stepping outside of consumerism, removing ourselves from the screen, and also beginning to conceive of objects and experiences beyond what they signal socially. This would mean becoming somewhat divorced from the systematised forms of approval that current technology facilitates, and to learn to love the way in which an object functions and the value that it might have accrued through decades of use and associated memory, but also learning to enjoy encounters for their own sake and with no other attendant accolade or cheer. If we want to start taking our world more seriously, it first requires us to stop reducing its many riches to opportunities to boost our own, hyper individual and abstracted cultural capital – our tradable identity or image that we project out into the world. Practical ways in which we might start to do this are the subject of another book. But it can begin by dispensing wherever possible with the tyrannies I have described here, and which make each of us – even those skilled in the art of consumerism and leisure – miserable for the fact that they always require upkeep. Again, and I want to stress this, it does not mean embracing any sort of 'bad taste' or brashness as an alternative, which only serves to reinforce the existence of such a binary and ends up creating new trends and strains of consumer desire which are ultimately as impoverished and harmful as the ones they replace.

Because, as our friends Frasier and Niles demonstrated, even the winners in this economy of professional appearances and qualifications are never free of the anxiety and dread caused by a system of intense and relentless competition, and this can extend to other forms of cultural capital, including coolness, relevance, or popularity. Trauma is a word that is overused but it is also apt here in describing the subtle but profound sadness of always having to strive and second-guess our own judgements, due to the approval that is necessitated by an economy of appearances and impressions.

In this respect, and in full knowledge of what an outlandish statement this might have seemed prior to reading the book, the fixation with taste constitutes a form of violence, and one that we are maybe all guilty of perpetrating at times as we are encouraged to exert whatever power is available to us. Ultimately it is one that ends up hurting us all – consigned, on top of everything else, to living out our few short years on this planet not just under the burden of financial insecurity and struggle, but in homes that are exclusively grey and austere, wearing functional clothes that allow us to pass undetected in the right circles and therefore stand the best chance of survival, eating food that is fetishised for its spareness and simplicity, reducing a whole world of infinite possibility to something called a 'bucket list' and being beholden to it at the expense of just doing whatever we feel like doing from one moment to the next. We risk not meeting the people who could become some of the most meaningful connections of our life, for fear that their dubious trainers or rucksacks might somehow infect us. It is an ick that is misplaced and ridiculous, that needs to be urgently discarded, unless we ourselves are happy to complete the work of capitalism and destroy whatever small pleasures are still available to us on earth.

Broken windows

In a final tribute to lovely Merle Oberon, who lived and thrived despite the pressures to conform to a Hollywood ideal, I made a visit, while writing this book, to the village of Haworth in Yorkshire, where the Brontës lived and worked. At the Brontë Parsonage Museum and protected behind glass, I saw items from the wardrobe of Charlotte Brontë, who, being the most successful of the sisters in their lifetime and the only one who really enjoyed the status of literary celebrity, also enjoyed the luxury of shopping. Among the fine gowns, parasols and moccasin shoes exhibited to showcase the extent of her worldliness and flair, which also corrected the myth told by popular TV and film programming that the Brontë clan were all somewhat drab and gothic, I came across an object that captured so much of what I was interested in and writing about. Called an 'ugly bonnet', it was an accessory popular among affluent women of the mid-to-late nineteenth century, and consisted of a concertina of fabric that was applied over the ordinary bonnet to protect it from the rain. Its name derived from the way that its functionality spoiled the simple elegance of women's fashions of the time. Nevertheless, the 'ugly', as it was often shortened to, became extremely fashionable, conforming to what we already know about the nineteenth-century tuxedo and the counter-intuitive developments that were taking place around clothing of the time, in which the most desirable items were often those that confounded traditional expectations of wealth and beauty. One can almost imagine Charlotte casually dropping into conversation mention of her 'ugly', to which the other sisters would have been forced to ask, 'your what?' before repeating the name back to themselves in disbelief.

Wuthering Heights (1847), and to a lesser extent *Jane Eyre* (1847), are themselves often accused of bad taste, having been characterised by some people in literary circles as sentimental, post-Romantic, Victorian chick-lit, unworthy of serious attention. And yet without even having to make appeals about the narrative prowess of both, and the adept handling of so much that I believe makes storytelling compelling and great (the unreliability of gossip and the fascination of status anxiety that is covered in both books), it is enough for me to say, after arguing the case over so many pages, that I love them both, and to close off with a reading of a text, and its film adaptation, that might very well inspire nausea in my critics.

As already stated, Merle's performance in the 1939 adaptation of *Wuthering Heights* haunted me when I first saw it, the overwrought expression of an actress indebted to the exaggerated theatrics of the silent-movie era perhaps, and specifically her strained, expressive eyes, imprinted a message about the harms of social mobility and self-improvement. While staying in Haworth and walking across the moors with my friend Joanne, we came to the realisation that *Wuthering Heights* the novel is really about the two forms of violence – the overt and the physical, and that which is more subtly encoded in ideas of good taste and respectability. In the book's oscillation between past and present is a struggle between the unruly tendencies of the younger Catherine and Heathcliff, and the forbidding cruelties of a society into which they will later be absorbed. There are many economic readings of the novel, but it is also the very particular social rules and cultural mores adjoining that economic narrative that interest me. The Earnshaws, to which Catherine belongs, are not a poor family after all, and much like the Sopranos a century and a half later, their wealth is nevertheless precarious and at risk of being lost through social faux pas.

The story of *Wuthering Heights* hinges on a scene in which the young Catherine and Heathcliff are caught peering through the window of a nearby mansion, Thrushcross Grange, owned by the wealthy and respectable Linton family. In the book, and relaying the incident to the housekeeper Nelly Dean, Heathcliff describes the home as being elegant, refined and in-keeping with the interior design fashions of the time: '... a splendid place carpeted with crimson, and crimson-covered chairs and tables, and a pure white ceiling bordered by gold, a shower of glass-drops hanging in silver chains from the centre, and shimmering with little soft tapers'. This is a deliberate counterpoint to Wuthering Heights the house, which is described as dark, disordered and, as it forms a sort of character within the book, unruly and unkempt. Regardless of the splendour, the inhabitants of Thrushcross Grange are in turmoil, as Catherine and Heathcliff witness the two children and heirs to the household arguing over the possession of a pet dog. In the film equivalent of that scene, what occurs inside Thrushcross Grange is a lavish dance attended by wealthy people who twirl and chatter.

Merle brings to the scene an added desperation and sadness as Catherine, fitfully adjusting her position to get a better look of the partygoers, and eyeing them with a joy that verges on the manic. After watching the guests dance about the room, identifying the type of dress she would wear and the type of coat that would best befit Heathcliff, she turns to her companion and with a raspy, yearning voice that was common to film actresses of the time, asks: 'Oh Heathcliff, *will we, will we ever?*'

To avoid being spotted, Catherine then ducks below the window causing a disturbance among the bushes below that alerts the estate's guard dogs, who chase the pair to the edge of the property where they are eventually caught and reprimanded by the owners.

Catherine comes to be embraced by the world witnessed through the window, while Heathcliff spends the rest of his days trying to disrupt it. The scene is not just pivotal to the story of *Wuthering Heights*, but in the social shifts that it describes, also our story. According to the trajectories of the novel's two central characters, the only options available to the lower orders would seem to be either pursuing this lifestyle by making incremental advances, seeking to prove themselves to the higher orders through fawning attempts at emulation, repressed desire and self-expression, in the way of Catherine, allowing this project to absorb them entirely and feeling a sense of shame towards everything they have ever known or been before – or else, in the way of Heathcliff, spurning it with a hatred that only contaminates their being.

But there is a third way out perhaps, albeit one that serves little purpose to the gothic novelist of the nineteenth century: of remaining nonplussed by whatever judgements are implied by that spectacle, of stepping away from the window altogether and never looking back; realising that we all present a similarly privileged image to someone, and to resist whatever urge we might have to wield these markers of our relative smarts, initiation, wealth or social dominance in order to soothe ourselves.

Windows are a powerful symbol used throughout *Wuthering Heights*, appearing like entry points, but more often serving as barriers to exclude. They are used to denote a character's insider, or outsider, status, most vividly of all, in the harrowing scene at the novel's start, where the spectre of Catherine calls through the window of the room at Wuthering Heights, asking to be let back in. As Catherine will later find out, albeit in bodily form, the world inside the Linton mansion is very different to the one observed from outside its window, which was really only a diorama or display.

Today our social worlds extend a little further than the bottom of the hill, and our private domains are often gleaned virtually. But the story illustrates a tendency that was just getting under way in the early nineteenth century, and with the opportunities for personal betterment that were being created, of pressing our noses up and breathing heavily on to the glass screen of another life that would seem, at least, much less ugly than our own.

Notes

Chapter One: Tastemakers

1. Johnson, Caitlin, 'Dolly: I Wanted To Grow Up To Be "Trash"', *CBS News* [website], 20 Dec 2006 cbsnews.com/news/dolly-i-wanted-to-grow-up-to-be-trash
2. 'And while the rugby is possibly thrilling for some, others were loving the look inside their living room – not least because it wasn't what many were expecting. "Did anyone else zoom in and try to have a nosey around their front room?!!!!" one person wrote, while another put, "Love to see that their TV watching room is as cluttered as the average [person]!"'
3. (Baxter-Wright, Dusty, 'Princess Anne's living room is surprising people', *Cosmopolitan*, 10 Feb 2021 cosmopolitan.com/uk/interiors/a35468630/princess-annes-living-room-surprising-reactions
4. Mears, Ashley, *Pricing Beauty: The Making of a Fashion Model*, Berkeley, 2011, p.75
5. Siegler, MG, 'Eric Schmidt: Every 2 Days We Create As Much Information As We Did Up To 2003', *TechCrunch* [news website], Aug 2010 tcrn.ch/bm9a2Q
6. Debord, Guy, *Society of the Spectacle*, Buchet-Chastel, 1967, p.2

Chapter Two: Homes

1. York, Peter, 'Trump's Dictator Chic', *Politico* Magazine [online], Mar/Apr 2017 politico.com/magazine/story/2017/03/trump-style-dictator-autocrats-design-214877
2. Employment figures, Creative Industries Council, Dec 2019, updated Feb 2021, thecreativeindustries.co.uk/facts-figures/uk-creative-overview-facts-and-figures-employment-figures
3. Bordieu, Pierre, Distinction: *A Social Critique of the Judgement of Taste*, originally published in France, 1979; translation published Routledge, 1984, p. 259
4. Ibid., p.277
5. Ibid., p.277
6. Hanley, Linsey, *Respectable: Crossing the Class Divide*, Penguin, 2017, p.16
7. Peterson, Anne Helen, 'The Company that Branded your Millenial Life is Switching to Burnout', *Buzzfeed*, 8 Oct 2019 buzzfeed.com/annehelenpetersen/millennial-burnout-startup-gin-lane-pattern-equal-parts

8. Abend, Lisa, 'How Kinfolk Magazine Defined the Millenial Asthetic ...
    and Unravelled Behind the Scenes', *Vanity Fair* [online magazine], 19 Mar
    2020 vanityfair.com/style/2020/03/how-kinfolk-magazine-defined-the-
    millennial-aesthetic-and-unraveled-behind-the-scenes
9. Debord, op. cit., p. 155
10. York, Peter, 'Trump's Dictator Chic', *Politico*, Mar 2017 politico.com/
    magazine/story/2017/03/trump-style-dictator-autocrats-design-214877
11. Debord, op. cit., p. 135

Chapter Three: Fashion

1. Estrada, Ryan, I'm sorry, I accidentally invented Normcore,
    Medium.com, 22 Nov 2014 medium.com/@ryanestrada/
    im-sorry-i-accidentally-invented-normcore-42e4f34732af
2. Sherman, Lauren, 'A Swan Song for the Philophiles', Business
    of Fashion, 1 Oct 2018 businessoffashion.com/articles/
    luxury/a-swan-song-for-the-philophiles
3. Book review: *The Quirks of Digital Culture* by David Beer',
    The London School of Economics and Political Science [review
    blog], 22 Mar 2020, blogs.lse.ac.uk/usappblog/2020/03/22/
    book-review-the-quirks-of-digital-culture-by-david-beer
4. Marks, Gene, 'The newest – and grossest – employee perk? Shoeless
    offices', *The Guardian*, 12 Dec 2019, theguardian.com/business/2019/
    dec/12/shoeless-offices-employee-perks

Chapter Four: Beauty

1. Illouz, Eva, *The End of Love: A Sociology of Negative Relations*, Polity,
    2021, p.205
2. Snow, Phillipa, *Which As You Know Means Violence*, Repeater, 2022,
    p.59
3. Lawrence, Andrew, 'She had to hide': the secret history of the first
    Asian woman nominated for a best actress Oscar, *Guardian*, 7 Mar 2023
    theguardian.com/film/2023/mar/06/merle-oberon-oscars-best-actress
4. Costello, Brid, 'Kate Moss: The Waif That Roared',
    Women's Wear Daily, 13 Nov 2009 wwd.com/feature/
    kate-moss-the-waif-that-roared-2367932-1410207

Chapter Five: Food

1. Bratskeir, Kate, '12 Ways Not To Spend Your Entire Life
    Savings At The Whole Foods Salad Bar', Huffington Post
    UK [online], 7 Dec 2017 huffingtonpost.co.uk/entry/
    whole-foods-salad-bar-win-it-you-can_n_5844160
2. Wilkinson, S. 'Blue Is The Warmest Colour Gets Its Very Own On-
    Point Parody', Grazia, 2 Jun 2021 graziadaily.co.uk/interiors/decoration/
    blue-warmest-colour-gets-point-parody
3. Dargis, Manohla, 'The Trouble with *Blue is the Warmest Colour*', *The New*

York Times [online], 27 Oct 2013 nytimes.com/2013/10/27/movies/the-trouble-with-blue-is-the-warmest-color.html

4. Walsh, Michael James; Baker, Stephanie Alice, 'What is emotional labour – and how do we get it wrong?' *The Conversation* [online], 11 Jul 2022 theconversation.com/what-is-emotional-labour-and-how-do-we-get-it-wrong-185773

5. Hatherley, Owen, *The Ministry of Nostalgia*, Verso, 2017, p.24

6. Brazier, Tori, Jamie Oliver felt 'threatened by food industry' while making Sugar Rush, *Metro* [online], 10 Mar 2022 metro.co.uk/2022/03/10/jamie-oliver-felt-threatened-by-food-industry-while-making-sugar-rush-16249004

7. Blair, Olivia, 'Nigella Lawson says she's "disgusted" by the term "clean eating"', *The Independent* [online], 9 Oct 2015 independent.co.uk/news/people/nigella-lawson-says-she-s-disgusted-by-the-term-clean-eating-a6687731.html

8. Hancox, Dan, 'The battle over bread', *Prospect* [online], 15 Jul 2019 prospectmagazine.co.uk/magazine/the-battle-over-bread

9. Lessing, Doris, *Memoirs of a Survivor*, Octagon Press, 1976, p.20

Chapter Six: Leisure

1. Evelyn Waugh is the other great author on this subject, and the 1980s TV adaptation of *Brideshead Revisited* starring Jeremy Irons is a must-watch for anyone interest in depictions of the leisure class.

2. 'Within each fraction, the second factor opposes those individuals whose families have long been members of the bourgeoisie to those who have recently entered it, the parvenus: those who have the supreme privilege, seniority in privilege, who acquired their cultural capital by early, daily contact with rare, "distinguished" things, people, places, and shows, to those who owe their capital to an acquisitive effort directed by the educational system or guided by the serendipity of the autodidact, and whose relationship to it is more serious, more severe, often more tense.' Quote from Bordieu, op cit, pp 261-2

3. Dyer, Geoff, *Yoga For People Who Can't Be Bothered To Do It*, Canongate, 2012

4. Dyer, Geoff, 'On My Radar: Geoff Dyer's cultural highlights', *The Guardian*, 30 Sep 2018 theguardian.com/culture/2018/sep/30/on-my-radar-geoff-dyer-burning-man-the-necks-luigi-ghirri

5. 'In a pre and post Covid world, I enjoy travelling and you can find me planning my next adventurous trip, whether that's a hike in Austria or a Tough Mudder race. I also like painting and sketching when I get the chance. Luckily a work/life balance is encouraged at Deloitte, giving me time to pursue my hobbies.' ('Deloitte Careers: The new world of cyber: Sanya's story', Deloitte [company website] www2.deloitte.com/uk/en/pages/careers/articles/the-new-world-of-cyber-sanyas-story.html

6. Partington, Richard, 'My Secret Life: Bear Grylls, adventurer, 35', *The Independent*, 1 May 2010 independent.co.uk/news/people/profiles/my-secret-life-bear-grylls-adventurer-35-1958216.html

7. Dowell, Ben, 'What's on TV and radio tonight: Tuesday, November 15', *The Times*, 15 Nov 2022 thetimes.co.uk/article/what-s-on-tv-and-radio-tonight-tuesday-november-15-c73ktlgbt

8. Altman, Anna, 'The Year of Hygge, the Danish Obsession with Getting

Cosy', *The New Yorker*, 8 Dec 2016 newyorker.com/culture/culture-desk/the-year-of-hygge-the-danish-obsession-with-getting-cozy

9. Fake Heiress Who Swindled New York's Elite Is Found Guilty', *The New York Times*, 25 Apr 2019 nytimes.com/2019/04/25/nyregion/anna-delvey-sorokin-verdict

10. 'A Fake Heiress Called Anna Delvey Conned the City's Wealthy. "I'm Not Sorry", She Says', *The New York Times*, 5 Oct 2019 nytimes.com/2019/05/10/nyregion/anna-delvey-sorokin

11. Deloache Williams, Rachel, 'As an Added Bonus, She Paid for Everything': My Bright-Lights Misadventure with a Magician of Manhattan, *Vanity Fair*, 13 Apr 2018

12. Hart, Jordan and Shamsian, Jacob, Infamous fake German heiress Anna Sorokin wins contempt case against ex-lawyer after landing guest speaking gig with Harvard MBA students, *Insider*, 26 Feb 2023 businessinsider.com/anna-sorokin-speak-harvard-mba-students-2023-2?r=US&IR=T

Chapter Seven: Abundance

1. 'As for the oft-quoted references to "piccaninnies" and "watermelon smiles", Johnson's remarks may have been in bad taste, but they were plainly satirical, and have been blown wildly out of proportion.' Gilligan, A., 'You've got the wrong Boris', *The Guardian*, 4 Sep 2007

2. Koncius, Jura, 'Marie Kondo's life is messier now – and she's fine with it', *The Washington Post*, 26 Jan 2023 washingtonpost.com/home/2023/01/26/marie-kondo-kurashi-inner-calm

Acknowledgements

This book was almost never written. The fact that it was, and the fact that you are now holding it in your hand, is thanks to Women's Aid and Refuge. I hope this goes some way to illustrating the transformative nature of their work, because there were times when I could barely find the courage to step outside the front door, let alone write confidently about my ideas. If you have a spare few pounds, please consider donating it to them.

Difficult times really do emphasise certain bonds, however, and there are many friends and loved ones who I must thank. First my mother Selina and stepfather Peter for being my one constant. Francisca, the counsellor who successfully dispelled the stubborn cruelties of a 90s state school system (!). My friends and neighbours Hamish, Alex and Grace. Sophie P for the intuition and constant friendship. Joanne for the midnight conversations and long rambles across the Yorkshire Dales. Camilla for the laughter that never stops and the reminder of how important it is for women to protect their imaginations. Lumi and her boys for their eternal hospitality. Lou and Ally for the many dinners and games. Rachael and Sophie C for their solidarity and wisdom. Leonie for the adventures. Becky for the art history and the very precious voice notes. Shon for the kindness and natural wit that shines through even the greyest of South London winters. Francisco, Lolly, Stan, Matty and Ryan for the weekly quiz. Sahil for the measured advice and sound judgement. Lauren for the laughs. Nina for being Nina. I love you all and will treasure the support you have given me forever.

Finally I need to thank my agent Emma, her assistant Monica, as well as Sharmaine and Hannah at Dialogue Books.

Bringing a book from manuscript to what you are reading is a team effort.

Dialogue Books would like to thank everyone who helped to publish *Bad Taste* in the UK.

Editorial
Sharmaine Lovegrove
Hannah Chukwu
Amy Mae Baxter
Jon Appleton

Contracts
Megan Phillips
Amy Patrick
Anne Goddard
Bryony Hall
Sasha Duszynska Lewis

Sales
Caitriona Row
Dominic Smith
Frances Doyle
Hannah Methuen
Lucy Hine
Toluwalope Ayo-Ajala

Design
Nico Taylor
Jo Taylor

Production
Narges Nojoumi

Operations
Kellie Barnfield
Millie Gibson
Sanjeev Braich

Publicity
Millie Seaward

Marketing
Emily Moran

Copy Editor
Saxon Bullock

Proofreader
Karyn Burnham